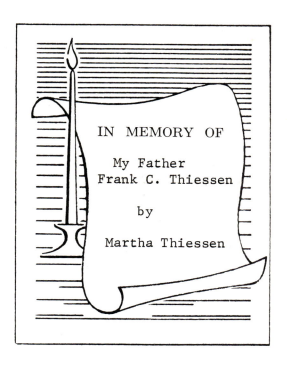

IN MEMORY OF

My Father
Frank C. Thiessen

by

Martha Thiessen

FRIEDRICH NIETZSCHE
By MAXIMILIAN A. MÜGGE

KENNIKAT PRESS
Port Washington, N. Y./London

FRIEDRICH NIETZSCHE

First published in 1912
Reissued in 1970 by Kennikat Press
Library of Congress Catalog Card No: 78-103207
SBN 8046-0844-X

Manufactured by Taylor Publishing Company   Dallas, Texas

CONTENTS

FRIEDRICH NIETZSCHE

INTRODUCTION

A PHILOSOPHER in the academical, in the technical sense
of the word Nietzsche was not. But if we accept his
own definition that " the real philosophers are com-
manders and law-givers," fighters against their time,
then *Nietzsche was a philosopher.*

A born artist, his training as a philologist merely increased Nietzsche's power as a master of form. There
are passages in his works, especially in *Thus Spake
Zarathustra,* which in beauty and grandeur rival the
psalms ; and the fascinating charm of his style, the
subtlety of his phrasing alone will ensure Nietzsche's
immortality. *Nietzsche was a poet-philosopher.*

Disillusioned by certain bitter experiences, oppressed
by the monotonous verbalism and the inevitable routine
of his duties as a professor of classical philology,
Nietzsche, then about thirty-four years of age, turned
from the study of words towards the study of facts.
He became a keen student of physiology for the remainder of his life; and henceforth his writings show a
wonderful blend of the culture of the aristocratic
classicist and the science of the hopeful biologist. True,
Nietzsche studied too much from books and too little
from life ; he was, scientifically speaking, just an
amateur in biology. This deficiency, however, is entirely outweighed by his unique hopefulness and by his
noble faith in the future of Man. Sir Francis Galton
himself, the founder of Eugenics, has shown no greater

faith and hope than Nietzsche, the apostle of the Superman. *Nietzsche was a pioneer of Eugenics.*—

His general attitude and the main problems with
which he was engaged may be summed up in the following propositions :

1. The world as a whole is amoral and without a
goal or purpose. It is an artistic phenomenon that will
recur eternally.

2. Hitherto mankind has had no goal either. A self-
set definite goal, however, is of artistic value and will
increase man's power. Such a goal is set before us by
the Superman, a higher and superior species of man.
The Superman is a life-furthering idea, the expression
of man's Will to Power.

3. Every religion, every system of morals or politics
which is hostile to life, which delays the coming of the
Superman must be abolished. Only the moral code of
strong and masterful men is compatible with the true
aims of life.

4. The Christian religion with its slave-morality is,
above all other, life's fiercest enemy. Christianity
counteracts Natural Selection. It is "the greatest of
all conceivable corruptions, the one immortal blemish
of mankind."

5. Our next goal, since the Superman will be but the
joy of a far-distant future, is to produce a higher and
superior race of men. These "Higher Men" will be,
however, only a transition to be followed and super-
seded by the new species, the Superman.

6. *The immediate steps advisable in a melioristic policy*
towards the "Higher Man" are : a Eugenics Revision
of our present marriage laws, a sensible education of
youth, a United Europe, and the annihilation of the
Christian Church.—

It is only possible within the scope of this small book
to touch upon a very few salient points in Nietzsche's
philosophy. The reader who desires to become better
acquainted with it must study his works. An excellent
English edition of them is now available, published in
eighteen volumes by Foulis. To the editor of this

translation, Dr. Levy, thanks are due for his kind permission to use various extracts in this book.

Nietzsche's health was rather indifferent and compelled him to write in snatches, and he often composed like a worker in mosaics. Only *The Birth of Tragedy*, *Thoughts out of Season*, *Thus Spake Zarathustra*, *The Genealogy of Morals*, *The Case of Wagner*, *The Antichrist*, and *Ecce Homo*—*i.e.* about half his works—consist of what is usually understood by coherent books. The other volumes contain over 4200 more or less—usually less !—connected aphorisms, and in addition a goodly number of essays, lectures, and fragments. The task of the systematising expositor is, therefore, made well-nigh impossible. The case for the defence is the worse, since, owing to Nietzsche's artistic and ever-changing temperament, there is scarcely any statement in his writing which is not contradicted by another somewhere. Yet it is hoped that the following exposition, which adheres as closely as possible to the poet-philosopher's words, is sufficiently coherent to make the reader perceive and appreciate Nietzsche's message.

Whatever his shortcomings are, they may be understood or forgiven if one considers the sheltered life Nietzsche led, that he never had to work hard, to " slave," that he had no insight into the lives and hearts of the humble and poor ; if one realises Nietzsche's frail health ; and, lastly, if one recalls the fact that he was a fighter, a fighter against his time, and that as such, rightly or wrongly, he often preferred the method of the cavalry attack to that of the sappers. Well, decidedly he has not solved the problems of the " Whither, Whence, and Why ? " We are still in Plato's den. But he has placed before our eyes a grand stimulating ideal, the *Superman*, the finest expression of that unswerving faith which we find in Swinburne's " Hymn on Man " :

" He hath stirred him, and found out the flaw in his fetters, and
　　cast them behind ;
　His soul to his soul is a law, and his mind is a light to his
　　mind.

The seal of his knowledge is sure, the truth and his spirit are
　　wed ;
Men perish, but man shall endure ; lives die, but the life is
　　not dead.

.　　　　.　　　　.　　　　.　　　　.

Glory to Man in the highest ! for Man is the master of
　　things ! "

CHAPTER I

NIETZSCHE'S LIFE

Name.—There is an adjective in the Czech language
which means " humble " and is spelt " nizky." There
is another adjective of the same meaning, " pokorny."
Many people in Germany are called Pokorny, but a
name more frequently found amongst those descendants
from Slavic forefathers is that of Nizky. This name
acclimatised appears under the most varied forms as
Nitzky, Nitzschky, Nitzschke, Nietzsche, all of which
can be found in directories.

Origin.—Our philosopher and his sister have recorded
a tradition that was much cherished by the former, and
certainly has contributed towards shaping the character of the proud aristocratic thinker. He believed
himself to be of noble origin. The Counts of Nietzki
who had to flee from Poland on account of their religious
beliefs, he considered to be his ancestors. So the boy
was told, and he believed it gladly. Indeed he said
one day, " A Count Nietzki must not lie."

Nobody has yet proved whether Nietzsche's cherished
belief is supported by facts or not. We do not know.
At any rate it is a remarkable coincidence that the
fiercest opponent of democracy, the haughtiest aristocrat, the apostle of everything that is *against* humility,
bore a name which means " the humble man." And
he, the apostle of the Antichrist, saw the light of day in
a German parsonage, the descendant of a generation of
parsons.

Birth.—Friedrich Nietzsche was born on the 15th

October 1844 in Röcken. His father, Karl Ludwig Nietzsche, was the pastor of this small solitary village situated in the Prussian province of Saxony. Karl Ludwig, the son and grandson of ecclesiastics, married Franziska Oehler, the daughter and granddaughter of parsons, on the 10th October 1843. Besides their firstborn child, the future poet-philosopher, they had two more children, a girl and a boy. Within two years of his birth the younger boy died. Elizabeth, however, was to survive even her famous eldest brother. She is still living to-day at Weimar, a rather too enthusiastic apologist of his philosophy, an eager chronicler of his life.

Early Childhood.—When Friedrich was scarcely four years of age, his father fell down a flight of steps. A concussion of the brain was the result. Whether this accident caused or accelerated the ensuing mental aberration of the reverend gentleman it is difficult to say. At any rate he lost his reason intermittently. He lingered on for a year till a merciful death released him. This sad event made a profound impression on the boy Friedrich.

Röcken, the village where he had spent the first four years of his life, lies in the neighbourhood of Naumburg. The latter was then a typical provincial town with almost medieval aspects, governed by narrow conventions and swayed by a clique of lawyers, officials, parsons, and old fogeys. The young widow had relatives living in Naumburg, so in 1850 she went there to stay with them.

Grave and serious beyond his years, the little Friedrich liked the sombre town, and his greatest ideal was to become a parson himself. And "the parson" his schoolfellows nicknamed him. One day it was raining hard, and the mother looked anxiously out of the window to see whether her boy was coming back from school. There he came round the corner, and, though he had neither overcoat nor umbrella, he was walking along very slowly, and with all the dignified bearing of an archbishop. When his mother reproachfully asked him why he did not run, he answered, almost shocked : " But, mother, our school regulations say that boys when coming from school are not to run in the street."

Though the boy had some playmates, his permanent companions within the house were his mother and sister, a grandmother, and two aunts. These feminine surroundings could not fail to exercise a definite influence upon him. Amongst its effects which may be traced throughout his life are his great sensitiveness, his fondness for self-inspection, and his ardent love for poetry and music.

He was the model of a good boy, but precocious. When about ten years of age he tried his skill at composing motets ; at twelve we find him writing several plays and many poems. Everybody in the house received at least a poem or a composition on her birth-day. Music became already quite a prominent factor in his life.

At School.—In Röcken the local schoolmaster and his father were the teachers of the young Nietzsche. After he left the elementary school at Naumburg, which he attended for scarcely a year, he spent several years at a private preparatory school, and in 1854 he entered the Gymnasium or the Grammar School at Naumburg.

The widow of the late Karl Ludwig Nietzsche, who had attained his pastorate through the direct help of King William of Prussia, was not without connections, and in 1858 she was offered a six-year scholarship for her son in the Landesschule at Pforta, a very ancient and famous public school.

Whereas the Grammar School at Naumburg is a day-school, Pforta is a boarding-school like our Harrow, only smaller. The curriculum was mainly classical, and a rather rigid discipline prevailed. This school has given many great men to Germany. Three well-known names may be instanced : Novalis, a poet and dreamer of lovely dreams ; Schlegel, a philologist and brilliant Shakespeare-scholar ; and Fichte, the great philosopher and patriot.

Friedrich Nietzsche became a scholar at Pforta in

October 1858. He was then fourteen years old. So many years had he lived under the softening home-influence of women that, now he had to take up residence at the College, he was not very happy at first. The routine and the discipline were not at all to his taste. He shrank from the other boarders, and very seldom went out. Once a week he left the cloistral silence of his school, but then only to meet his mother and his sister.

The boys had long hours, and were obliged to work hard. Practically nothing in the way of real sport brightened their daily routine, though occasional excursions and some swimming brought a little variety into their lives, which were regulated towards the one goal, to produce great scholars.

When the monotony of the daily studies, the pressure of discipline—which even during such excursions never wholly relaxed—weighed too heavily on him, the young Nietzsche found some consolation in writing down what he saw, felt, and hoped. He kept a kind of diary. The study of these youthful jottings is exceedingly interesting, since they reveal to us the boy's tendency for self-examination and self-contemplation. Sometimes they are decidedly premature and full of morbid sentiments—premature, when the boy of fourteen talks about the three periods or stages of his poetical work ; and morbid, when shortly after, because his birthday has passed once more, he talks about time passing like the rose of spring. Of the greatest import, however, are lines which show how the young thinker gradually loses the belief of his fathers. He does not break away suddenly ; but the writings of his favourite authors, Schiller, Hölderlin, Byron, and the higher criticism expounded by one or two of his masters, did not fail to pervade the young mind. Slowly he hauled up the anchors of his life's ship to leave the moorings of the authoritative creed of two thousand years' standing, and sailed forth without guide or compass on the Ocean of Doubt.

The brightest periods of Nietzsche's life at this time

were his holidays. Sometimes he would spend them with his people at Naumburg, sometimes he would stay with relatives or acquaintances. So we find him a visitor at Jena, at Dresden, and in the Harz mountains.

During his last year at the ancient school his life was happy, since the discipline was not so exacting towards the top-form boys, and since he had developed a certain easygoing indifference. One day he dined with one of the professors, another day he improvised on the piano for his friends. The literary society, "Germania," which he and his friends had founded, exercised much influence on him.

Nietzsche was brilliant in Scripture, German, and Latin, good in Greek, but weak in Mathematics—so his leaving certificate tells us. He left Pforta in September 1864, and shortly afterwards, together with his friend Deussen, he went to the University of Bonn.

At the University.—The students in a German university lead on the whole a very independent and gay life, the remembrance of which never dies, and often sheds a soothing light over the evening of old age. At first the boisterous and rollicking habits of his jolly fellow-students attracted Nietzsche. He became just one of the beer-drinking, singing, and duelling crowd for a time. But the schoolmaster and the parson were still powerful in him. Soon he began to hate the drinking bouts in the evening, the dawdling and courting in the streets, and withdrew more and more to his studies and his favourite recreation, music.

Philology and divinity were the subjects he studied during the first six months, then he abandoned the latter and devoted himself exclusively to philology. He attended various classes, and amongst his teachers mention might be made of Sybel, Jahn, and Ritschl.

Nietzsche's fellow-students named him " Sir Gluck " on account of his musical leanings. He often had to conduct small musical affairs in his club, the Franconia. The great musical festivals in the neighbouring Cologne were days of ecstasy to him.

More and more he turned away from the Christian

beliefs, and one can imagine the horror of the respectable Mrs. Nietzsche when, during the Easter holidays 1865, her son refused to go, as they were accustomed to do, to the Lord's Table. Later he wrote to his sister who was worrying about him : " If you desire peace of soul and happiness, believe ! if you want to be a disciple of truth, search ! "

In the autumn Nietzsche went to the University of Leipsic. The estrangement from his fellow club-members had become more and more pronounced, and his favourite professor, Ritschl, had gone to Leipsic. For two years Nietzsche studied hard at classical philology. He attended the lectures of the professors Curtius, Roscher, Tischendorf, and Ritschl. None of them, however, was fonder of the clever and wayward young student than the last mentioned. Without Ritschl the sudden meteor-like official career of Nietzsche would never have been possible.

During these two years at Leipsic, Nietzsche became acquainted with the writings of Schopenhauer. He was fascinated by the grim sage, whose masterpiece, *The World as Will and as Idea*, revolutionised the young man's outlook on life, and completed his separation from Christianity. Traces of Schopenhauer's doctrines can be found in all the books Nietzsche has written.

His private life at Leipsic was pleasant. He moved within a circle of sympathetic and congenial friends, visited his favourite professors, went to the theatres, roamed about the country, and had on the whole a very good time.

Military Service.—When still at Pforta, Nietzsche had trouble with his eyes. But though he was now actually short-sighted, he had in 1867 to fulfil the obligation of one year's military service. It was against his expectations and wishes. But the Prussian army needed more recruits, and the authorities enrolled even men who were usually exempted. The young scholar made the best of a bad job. After a short time of service in the 4th Regiment of the Field Artillery at Naumburg, he turned out quite a good soldier, and he was very proud to have been noted as the best rider in his detachment. His experiences as a soldier, together with that tradition of the Nietzsches as to their noble origin, have probably contributed towards his later aggressive, often haughty attitude, his fondness of war and of aristocracy.

He had been serving but a few months when an accident put a stop to his further military career. Whilst mounting his horse he lacerated some pectoral muscles. An operation was necessary. He recovered, and though he had to remain in Naumburg till the end of his year there was no more active service to be done, and he could devote his time to serious studies. On leaving he received the commission of a lieutenant of the reserve.

Further Studies.—Returning to Leipsic he continued his studies, and the brilliancy and thoroughness of his philological work endeared him still more to his teacher, Professor Ritschl. It was the latter who brought the young man completely under the influence of antiquity. Pforta had done much in that direction, but it was Ritschl who planted in him the fervent love of Grecian culture. It was Ritschl who protected him to a great extent against a certain desire to know everything and so to fritter away his strength. To be an absolute master in *one* subject was, owing to Ritschl's influence, henceforth, for some time at any rate, Nietzsche's ideal. Besides the influence of Ritschl and of Grecian antiquity, two other factors were responsible during those years at Leipsic for forming Nietzsche's personality. Reference has already been made to Schopenhauer. The other was Wagner.

All his life long Nietzsche was fond of music. At this time he became acquainted with Wagner's music, and shortly afterwards with the great master himself. The powerful personality of the famous composer completely enchanted the young enthusiast, and made him a most fervent admirer and follower of the wizard.

Professor at Bâle.—A great surprise awaited Nietzsche. The chair of Classical Philology in the University of

Bâle was vacant. Ritschl had been approached by the Bâle authorities for advice as to a suitable person. He recommended Nietzsche and wrote to the Senate : " He will be able to do anything he wants." And the young scholar, only twenty-four years of age, was appointed Professor of Classical Philology in the University of Bâle. He had not yet taken his doctor's degree. The philosophical faculty at Leipsic did not want to examine their colleague of Bâle, and they conferred on him the doctor's degree in recognition of his work and his philological treatises already published. On the 28th May 1869 Professor Friedrich Nietzsche delivered his inaugural lecture, entitled " Homer and Classical Philology."

His initial salary was about £120. That was not much, but he had inherited some money. His aunt Rosalie had left him a legacy in order to enable him to go in for an academical career, and an uncle of his, who had made a fortune in England, benefited all the Nietzsches. His University duties were light. There were the usual lectures, but only eight students, which comprised the total of the philologists at the small University. In addition to these duties he had to teach Greek to the boys of the top form of the chief public school at Bâle, the Pädagogium.

With these boys Nietzsche was on the best of terms. He used to prefer a difficult text to the usual routine reader, and his teaching was more intensive than extensive ; he would rather bestow his attention on a gifted boy to perfect him, and leave the average and weak boy to work out his own salvation.

The people at Bâle are of a reserved character, and the young professor often felt lonely at first. Soon, however, he to whom hero-worship seems to have been second nature was to be happy. In August 1869 Nietzsche wrote to a friend : " I have found a man who personifies to me as no one else does that which Schopenhauer calls ' the genius,' and who is entirely pervaded with that wonderful heart-stirring philosophy. Such an absolute idealism prevails in him, such a deep and stirring humanism, such a lofty seriousness of life, that in his neighbourhood I feel as near something divine." And—in 1888 Nietzsche called Wagner a " clever rattlesnake, a typical decadent " !

While still a student at Leipsic Nietzsche had been introduced to Wagner, and was asked to call when an opportunity should offer itself. The mighty master of music had established his domicile at Tribschen, not far from Luzern, in order to complete his great trilogy. Scarcely a month after his arrival the new professor paid a visit to Wagner. The result was that the youthful enthusiast enlisted amongst the fighters for Wagner's cause, whose music and whose plan of a great national opera-house had at that time innumerable enemies in Germany. Wagner had a considerable influence over his young friend, and many of Nietzsche's later ideas were the fruit of seed sown in those days. Many a pleasant week-end was spent at Tribschen. By Christmas 1869 he was already such an intimate friend of the family that Cosima, Wagner's wife, commissioned him to buy Christmas gifts for the children and others.

The War.—In July 1870 war between France and Germany broke out. On becoming a Swiss professor Nietzsche had also to become a Swiss subject. Nevertheless he, who later on was to become the arch-enemy of narrow national ideals, asked his authorities for leave to go to the front as a nurse. The permission was given. He obtained a short course of training, and was sent out with many orders which he successfully executed. Whilst in charge of a convoy of wounded soldiers whom he accompanied to Germany, he contracted from them dysentery and diphtheria. His war-career was ended. The impression, too, of the horrors he had seen had been almost too much for him. He never would talk about it.

After he was only partially recovered, he went back to Bâle and took up his duties again. It did not last long, and he had to pay the penalty of his daring campaign as nurse and for not allowing his ailments to be completely cured. He fell ill, suffering from violent neuralgia, insomnia, eye-troubles, and indigestion. Two months' rest at Lugano, however, were sufficient to restore him to health.

"**Birth of Tragedy.**"—Meanwhile his first book, *The Birth of Tragedy*, was nearing completion. At first he could not find a publisher at all, but during the last days of 1871 it appeared in print. It was an homage paid to Wagner. The keynote of this book is perhaps : " Only as an æsthetic phenomenon existence and the world appear justified " ; and, " Art supplies man with the necessary veil of illusion which is required for action. For the true knowledge as to the awfulness and absurdity of existence kills action." Nietzsche opposes the Greek culture existing *before* and *after* Socrates. The former civilisation was intoxicated with its myths, its Dionysian songs ; it was strong, cruel, grand ; the latter was impious, rationalistic, bloodless, feeble. The author goes on to say that the culture of his time is on the whole too much like that of the past Socratian period, but that salvation will come if the bidding of Wagner's great mystic music is followed. Many other interesting points are discussed. The book is one of the few comparatively well constructed and coherent books which Nietzsche has written, and the beginner should commence his study of Nietzsche with this or with *Thoughts out of Season*, but on no account with *Thus Spake Zarathustra* or one of the numerous books of aphorisms.

Naturally the maestro and his wife hailed the book with the greatest delight ; but the general public ignored it, and no reviewer took it up. The philologists, Nietzsche's professional colleagues, shrugged their shoulders. One of them, a professor in Bonn, informed his students that *The Birth of Tragedy* was " pure nonsense." Another philologist wrote a vitriolic and abusive pamphlet against Nietzsche's book. Though one of his old and intimate friends, Rohde, published a brilliant counter-attack to that pamphlet, Nietzsche felt depressed. For a time he was professionally

tabooed, and students were advised not to go to Bâle
to study philology.

Another cause of sadness was added : Wagner left
Tribschen for Bayreuth, where the great National
Opera-House was being erected.   Yet Nietzsche's old
philological reputation was still great enough to bring
some sunshine into these days.   The Universities of
Greifswald and of Dorpat each wanted the young
professor for themselves.   We must presume that *The
Birth of Tragedy* had not reached the authorities.
Nietzsche refused both offers.   The Bâle Senate increased his salary to £158 11*s*. in recognition of his
loyalty.

An untiring worker was Nietzsche. He attended to
his official duties, he gave public lectures, and wrote
several philological papers.   The public lectures on
" The Future of our Educational Institutions," which
he gave in 1872, are very interesting.   He fights against
the shallow education of the masses, the useless specia-
lisation in philological circles.   Two kinds of schools
he distinguishes—institutions for giving culture, and
institutions for teaching how to succeed in life.   The
latter do not interest him much ; his ideal is culture,
which should consist " above all in obedience and
habituation."   " Let no one hope to reach sound
æsthetic judgments along any other road than the
thorny one of language, and by this I do not mean
philological research, but self-discipline in one's mother-
tongue."

" **Thoughts out of Season.**"—From 1873–6 in quick
succession Nietzsche published four long essays which
he called *Thoughts out of Season*.   The first one, entitled
" David Strausz, the Confessor and the Writer," was a
fierce indictment of Strausz, a popular free-thinker,
then much in vogue, and of the shallow self-sufficiency
of the Germans after the war.   " Culture-Philistines "
Nietzsche calls these Germans whose culture has contentment written in its every feature.   The second
essay, " The Use and Abuse of History," was a bitter
attack on his contemporaries and those professors of

history who make historic learning an idol. "We would serve history only so far as it serves life, but to value its study beyond a certain point mutilates and degrades life," says the author, and " the unrestrained historical sense, pushed to its logical extreme, uproots the future, because it destroys illusions and robs existing things of the only atmosphere in which they can live." The third essay, " Schopenhauer as Educator," extols Schopenhauer as *the* great philosopher, and as the model and type of future man, and goes for the servile state-paid university professor of philosophy. The last and fourth essay of this group, " Richard Wagner in Bayreuth," too, is a eulogy. " The enterprise at Bayreuth signifies in the realm of art, so to speak, the first circumnavigation of the world, and by this voyage not only was there apparently new art discovered, but Art itself." And of Wagner's poetry our author says : " There is a heartiness and candour in his treatment of the German language scarcely to be met with in any other German writer, save perhaps Goethe." And Nietzsche's summing-up words on Wagner are : " No artist of what past soever has yet received such a remarkable portion of genius."

Nietzsche called these four essays *Thoughts out of Season*, because he tried to represent various things— of which his age was somehow proud—as faults and defects. The language of these four essays is often very bitter, and it is no great wonder that the number of Nietzsche's enemies grew, and that, from the publisher's as well as from the author's point of view, the result was *nil*.

The Breach with Wagner.—" Richard Wagner in Bayreuth " was a kind of farewell. For some years the two friends had been drifting from one another. True, Nietzsche did all he could with his pen and his purse to bring about the success of Bayreuth. But all the time he was suspicious that he was only regarded as a Wagnerite, and not estimated for himself. Wider and wider the estrangement grew, though neither of the two showed it as yet. Wagner without doubt did look on Nietzsche sometimes as his tool, but what genius does not use for his purposes every man he meets? At the same time Wagner was kind to his young friend, and took a real and personal interest in him. If Nietzsche had followed Wagner's advice, " Marry, and then *travel!* " who knows whether we should not have had a greater Nietzsche?

Shortly after Christmas, 1875, his health broke down again, but once more, after a short journey for recuperation, his constitution triumphed. A pathetic element entered Nietzsche's life in April. He fell in love with a charming young Dutch lady, Miss Tr. He asked her to be his wife, and she refused since her heart was given to someone else. It took Nietzsche some time to get over that.

On the 12th July 1876 Wagner thanked his friend for the fourth volume of *Thoughts out of Season* with the words, " My friend, your book is tremendous! " and he invited him over to Bayreuth. It was the last letter Wagner ever addressed to Nietzsche. The first performance of the *Ring of the Nibelungen* took place soon afterwards. Nietzsche went, not sure of himself—nor of anything.

Wagner was charmed that success had come to him at last. A brilliant company had assembled to attend the first performances. The Emperor, a king, financiers, snobs, counts, writers, everybody was there, and the Master was the idol of most of them. This powerful ruler of masses and cliques was no longer to Nietzsche the kind and sympathetic friend of Tribschen. Besides, the glowing imagination of the poet-thinker had always cherished too ideal expectations about his musical idol, about the performances and the audiences. The reality he encountered was ever so different. Everything disgusted him, and he left Bayreuth.

A great change came over him. From an enthusiastic " Dionysian " dreamer he turned into a calm " Apollonian " thinker; he began to distrust art and metaphysics, and to place his faith more in science and research. The scholar prevailed over the artist. Or, to put it in a different way, during the period that he wrote *Human, All-too-human*, *The Dawn of Day*, and *Joyful Wisdom*, Nietzsche, whom, during all the remainder of his literary activity, the label poet-philosopher fits best, might be suitably called a philosopher-poet.

His health once again grew worse, and necessitated a year's vacation. With two friends—of whom the one, Rée, certainly influenced Nietzsche towards becoming a determinist by drawing his attention to the English school of philosophy—he went to Naples, where all three stayed in the house of Miss Meysenbug, a good and experienced society lady and authoress. They had a happy time together. Over six months passed. Then, after a cure at a watering-place, Nietzsche went back to Bâle and again resumed his professional duties.

"**Human, All-too-human.**"—He continued, too, his work as an author. But his failing health made it impossible for him to write continuously and to adhere to any one plan for a long time. Henceforth *the aphorism became his favourite vehicle of thought*. He was fond of comparing aphorisms with mountain-peaks, and of stating that in the mountains the shortest way is from peak to peak, but that for such a route one must have "long legs and be big and tall."

Most of his thoughts occurred to him during his long and solitary walks. He jotted down a few notes which, it is true, he polished and perfected often with admirable patience and ability, but his health did not allow him to construct the *well-designed* mosaic of a beautiful book out of his polished stones. In his *Dawn of Day* Nietzsche says : " A book like this is not intended to be read through at once or to be read aloud. It is intended more particularly for reference, especially on our walks and travels ; we must take it up and put it down again after a short reading." This certainly applies to the two volumes of *Human, All-too-human* and likewise to *The Dawn of Day* and to *The Joyful Wisdom*.

In May 1878 the *first* volume of *Human, All-too-human* appeared, a collection of over six hundred aphorisms. Wagner and his followers condemned or ignored the book, for a new Nietzsche had written this. He who formerly abused Socrates now lauded him. Now we read : " It is a mark of a higher culture to value the little unpretentious truths, which have been found by means of strict method, more highly than the joy-diffusing and dazzling errors which spring from meta-physical and artistic times and peoples." Nietzsche has become a determinist. He denies the freedom of will.

One group of aphorisms in this volume may be placed on a level with Stevenson's *Art of Writing*, with Sir Philip Sidney's *A Defence of Poetry*. It is entitled, " Concerning the Souls of Artists and Authors," and reveals the marvellous depths of Nietzsche's artistic temperament and psychological insight. Similar magnificent aphorisms on writing and writers are to be found in the second volume of *Human, All-too-human*, and also in *Joyful Wisdom*.

More and more Nietzsche found his own way, his own philosophy, himself. Schopenhauer and Wagner were discarded, and he called *Human, All-too-human*, of which the second volume appeared in two parts in 1879–80, " the monument of a crisis." This second volume, a collection of over seven hundred aphorisms, is likewise under the sway of Socrates. " The time will come when men will take up the Memorabilia of Socrates rather than the Bible." Written for free spirits, the text like a magic carpet carries the reader through the valleys and over the heights of human thought, and the author, our guide, keeps us decidedly in good humour, especially when he dismisses us smilingly with the words, " We should not let ourselves be burnt for our opinions —we are not so certain of them as all that. But we might let ourselves be burnt for the right of possessing and changing our opinions."

Nietzsche's eyes, stomach, and head were the demons that never let him alone. Worse and worse grew his health until finally he broke down completely, and in 1879 he had to resign his professorship. The Senate, in a very gracious letter, thanked him for his services, and granted him a pension equivalent to his initial salary.

He went to St. Moritz, in the Ober-Engadine, and slowly recovered a little, so that he could even work sometimes at the second part of his *Human, All-too-human*. But it was a respite only. By Christmas of that year his sufferings were almost unbearable, and he thought death was near.

Yet he lived through it, and when in the following spring he stayed at Venice, the wonderful city had the most beneficent influence on him. Henceforth, we find him a solitary and restless wanderer, dividing his time between Italy, the Engadine, and Germany. He spent least of his time in Germany, most in Italy, but he loved the Engadine. For years we see him drifting from place to place, either searching for health and friends, or for solitude and truth. He stayed nowhere very long, with the exception of Venice, Genoa, Nice, and Sils-Marie in the Engadine.

He led a most frugal life. When lodging in Genoa he prepared his simple meals himself on a spirit-lamp. Sometimes in the evenings headaches would torment him, and without lighting up he stretched himself out on the sofa. " He is too poor to burn candles," said his neighbours, so they offered him some. He thanked the kind souls, and explained, but they called him " Il Santo," the Saint.

The mornings he spent in long solitary walks along the sea-coasts or in the mountains ; sometimes, when the sun was too hot, he would rest, lizard-like, lazily in the sun, always thinking and dreaming. His notebook was his constant companion.

" **The Dawn of Day.**"—In 1881 another book was completed, *The Dawn of Day*. The preceding book was to some extent a transitional work ; now he wanted to indicate the dawn of his own, his very own, philosophy. Again we find a vast mass of aphorisms dealing with almost every possible subject, and on the whole they are excellent for their insight into human nature. Very marked is the author's hostile attitude towards Christianity. " Would he not be a cruel god if, being himself in possession of the truth, he could calmly contemplate mankind in a state of miserable torment, worrying its mind as to what was truth ? " " Christianity has developed into soft moralism." As we said before, Rée had drawn Nietzsche's attention to the English materialists, and their influence, which was already perceptible in the previous book, becomes very clear in *The Dawn of Day*. " *It is only from the sciences of physiology and medicine that we can borrow the foundation-stones of new ideals.*" Nietzsche had become a pioneer of Eugenics !

For Spencer, however, he had but scant respect. The disciple of Empedocles, Heraclitus, and Goethe, Nietzsche tried hard to look at Nature without juggling into it finality or a purpose. On the majestic and rocky heights of Sils-Marie the thought of the Eternal Recurrence occurred to him and slowly crystallised. Everything happens again, everything returns, even this day, this book, and its reader. Nietzsche was quite excited about what he thought a discovery. Of course needlessly, for, in the first place, the idea is almost as ancient as mankind itself ; and, secondly, it is a sterile idea, and if it were true, the sooner we dynamite the earth the better. The fact of the matter is, the keen intellectual atmosphere in which the Apollonian author of *Human, All-too-human* lived was dimmed again by the haze coming down from the mountainous realms of Dionysian fancies.

" **The Joyful Wisdom.**"—The influence of this sad metaphysical idea, the Eternal Recurrence, began to depress him. Once more, however, the sun broke through ; he revelled in the music of *Carmen*, and in 1882 he gave to the world one of the brightest books he has ever written, *The Joyful Wisdom*. One cannot better characterise this life-pulsing, life-loving, and vigorous aphorism-book than by quoting some lines from one of the poems which it contains :

A DANCING SONG TO THE MISTRAL.

Wildly rushing, clouds outleaping,
Care-destroying, Heaven sweeping,
   Mistral wind, thou art my friend !
Surely 'twas one womb did bear us,
Surely 'twas one fate did pair us,
   Fellows for a common end.

Dance, oh ! dance on all the edges,
Wave-crests, cliffs and mountain ledges,
   Ever finding dances new !
Let our knowledge be our gladness,
Let our art be sport and madness,
   All that's joyful shall be true !

Sweep away all sad grimaces,
Whirl the dust into the faces
   Of the dismal sick and cold !
Hunt them from our breezy places,
Not for them the wind that braces,
   But for men of visage bold.

It is a cheerful book, and a fine performance of the artist Nietzsche. The disheartening idea of the Eternal Recurrence is displaced by the more stimulating vision of the Superman. Zarathustra is mentioned for the first time.

"**Thus Spake Zarathustra.**"—Following a whim, Nietzsche travelled in the spring of 1882 to Sicily. He intended to spend the whole summer in Messina, but a few sirocco-days were sufficient to drive him away. He accepted an invitation of Miss Meysenbug to come to Rome. She evinced an almost maternal interest in the personality and the genius of Nietzsche. She wanted to find him a companion, a wife. Besides, had he not written once to her, " I tell you in confidence, what I need is a good woman." Now Miss Meysenbug believed she had found her who would prove a worthy companion and disciple of the roaming philosopher. The young girl, Lou-Salomé, was scarcely twenty years of age. Nietzsche fell in love with her at once, and after a time proposed and—was refused. They remained friends for some months nevertheless, but their friendship came to a sudden end. What exactly happened behind the scenes throughout all this time no one knows, since the only surviving actors, Lou-Salomé and Nietzsche's sister, naturally do not tell us clearly and openly all the facts and intrigues of what seems to have been a tragi-comedy. It was just a human episode. Not only had Nietzsche lost the prospect of the best friend a man ever can have, a good wife, but he also lost his friend Rée through this affair, because he thought him guilty of treachery.

More lonely than ever, he set out again on his wanderings. And now his love concentrates on his spiritual child, Zarathustra, the central hero of his next book, *Thus Spake Zarathustra*, the finest dream-creation of the artist Nietzsche. The blind, hopeless mechanism of the Eternal Recurrence no longer satisfies him. He wants to posit a human goal, to eulogise action, to ennoble man through the ideal of the superman. "*I teach you the Superman*. Man is something that is to be surpassed. What have ye done to surpass man? All beings hitherto have created something beyond themselves, and ye want to be the ebb of that great tide, and would rather go back to the beast than surpass man? The Superman is the meaning of the earth. Let your will say : The Superman *shall* be the meaning of the earth ! I conjure you, my brethren, remain true to the earth, and believe not those who speak unto you of super-earthly hopes ! " With that joyous note does the book open, with that gospel Zarathustra comes down from his mountains.

The work consists mostly of addresses or sermons which Zarathustra delivers to an imaginary audience. A very vague story-plot threads these sermons together. That Nietzsche gave the name of the famous Persian sage Zoroaster to his hero was at first a mere fancy, though later on he insinuated various meanings into the name. The first half of the book has as its central idea the Superman; then, however, sets in again the idea of the Eternal Recurrence. It is true, in his auto-biography Nietzsche calls the Eternal Recurrence the fundamental idea of his work. Nevertheless it is a pity he brought it into *Thus Spake Zarathustra*, which without it would be the song of songs of Eugenics, though it is a fragment. Once more in the chapter on "Old and New Tables," a sort of epitome of his leading doctrines, the poet-philosopher soars high on the wings of hope for his Superman, but soon he terms himself again the teacher of the Eternal Recurrence, and the beautiful Superman-idea becomes clouded by that accursed Eternal Recurrence, its very antithesis. The discord is hopeless. Nietzsche himself must have felt it, for he certainly *planned* a continuation of his vague plot, and perhaps a reconciliation of those two ideas. As it stands, his masterpiece is a grand and beautiful torso.

The book consists of four parts. They were written and published successively during 1883 and 1884. The quaint work, with its peculiar mixture of unique and personal reminiscences, did not appeal to his contem-poraries, and had no sale. The fourth part was therefore printed privately at Nietzsche's expense, and in forty copies only, which he intended to distribute amongst his friends. It is a proof of his extreme loneliness that he could only muster seven people to whom he could send a copy. Practically no reviewer, no critic, took any notice of what Nietzsche later called the deepest book and the greatest gift that has ever been bestowed upon men.

Sometimes an enthusiastic reader would come and visit the lonely philosopher. So did Heinrich von Stein, Paul Lanzky, and others; but they soon drifted again out of the life of the man who was dying for faithful friends and disciples, and yet never could manage to keep the few whom life and chance brought across his path.   And then he dreamt of a convent-like coterie of superior men as his friends, to be guided by him—a kind of Port-Royal.

"**Beyond Good and Evil.**"—Plan after plan as to his next book now followed, and his notebooks were crammed with ideas.   Sometimes he thought of the construction of a great work which was to embody in a system the whole of his philosophy.   It was never finished.   But he used and elaborated part of his notes, and wrote a " Prelude to a Philosophy of the Future " under the title *Beyond Good and Evil.*   He could not find a publisher ;   the public did not want his books. At last he decided to have it published at his own expense ;   in 1886 it appeared.   Again a collection of about three hundred aphorisms, it has many points in common with *The Joyful Wisdom.*   It is a bright, subtle, and wayward work written for " free, very free, spirits."   The attacks on philosophers and scholars are evidence of great psychological insight, and the last chapter of aphorisms, " What is Noble ? " is truly elevating.   Interesting is his attitude of super-nationalism ; for he glorifies a United Europe, and in his judgments on the various nations the English fare very badly : " They are a fundamentally mediocre species . . . ponderous, conscience-stricken, herding animals . . . the English mechanical stultification of the world. . . . Shakespeare, that marvellous Spanish-Moorish-Saxon synthesis of taste, over whom an ancient Athenian of the circle of Æschylus would have half-killed himself with laughter or irritation . . . the absurd muddle-head Carlyle . . . herd of drunkards and rakes . . . the plebeianism of modern ideas is England's work and invention."

But in private life Nietzsche was gentle and amiable. We have the testimony of all those who met the lonely philosopher year in, year out, at Sils-Marie to that effect.   An English lady of delicate health once said to him, "I know you are a writer, Mr. Nietzsche. I should like to read your books."   And Nietzsche, who knew her to be a devoted Catholic, said : " No, I don't want you to read them. If what I publish be true, a feeble woman like you would have no right to exist." But these well-inclined hotel acquaintances were not real friends ; a terrible loneliness, now more than ever, was Nietzsche's fate.

" **The Will to Power.**"—Again he tackles his intended great systematical work. The title is to be *The Will to Power ; An Attempted Transvaluation of All Values.* During the winter 1886, at Nice, he also re-edited *The Birth of Tragedy, Dawn of Day,* and *Joyful Wisdom,* and wrote those remarkable prefaces which give us many a hint as to the spiritual Odyssey of the poet-philosopher.

In the beginning of 1887 Nietzsche became acquainted with a certain Madame v. P. We know little about this affair, not even the name of the lady. Certain it is, however, that they went together to San Remo and Monte Carlo.

His health troubled him again, and he had to give himself up to the doctors at Coire in Switzerland, but all the time the vision of his great theoretical work was hovering before him, and schemes and headings of chapters were thought out. But, as already stated, this *opus magnum* was never completed. His failing health and various other causes made it impossible. He probably saw that himself, and so he published small parts of his notes as separate books. *Beyond Good and Evil,* and all the books after that, with the exception of *The Case of Wagner* and of his auto-biography, are nothing but such prematurely published and elaborated notes.

Amongst the papers which have appeared in print since Nietzsche's death the reader will find the notes intended to furnish the material for that large work, *The Will to Power.* In the English edition they fill two volumes of over 800 pages. They make one feel extremely sorry that the artist-philosopher was never able to complete that systematical work of his which occupied his thoughts from 1883–89. It was to prove that the Will to Power is the Life-principle and not

the Struggle for Existence ; it was to fight Socialism—
" the tyranny of the meanest and the most brainless "—
to refute Christianity, to attack the English philosophers
—that " blockhead, John Stuart Mill " and " Herbert
Spencer's tea-grocer's philosophy "—and to prepare the
way for the Superman : to mention only a few of
the items out of many. Of the best quality are surely
the epistemological passages to be found under " The
Will to Power in Science," the two or three Eugenics
passages under " Society and the State," and some
passages under " The Order of Rank."

" **Genealogy of Morals.**"—A certain Swiss critic attacked Nietzsche's work, *Beyond Good and Evil*, and,
calling it " a text-book of anarchism," designated it as
dynamite.   Within a few weeks Nietzsche wrote three
polemic essays as an elucidation to *Beyond Good and
Evil*, and published them in 1887 under the title *The
Genealogy of Morals*.   They deal with the problems :
" Under what conditions did Man invent for himself
those judgments of values, ' Good ' and ' Evil ' ?   And
what intrinsic value do they possess in themselves ? "
They contain many shrewd conjectures as to the origin
and evolution of guilt, bad conscience, and punishment,
and also fierce onslaughts on Wagner.   The preface,
written at Sils-Marie, towards the end, with Nietzsche's
self-laudation, is a peculiar indication of the author's
incipient mental unbalance.

In October 1887 we find him in Nice.   Two incidents
mark his stay at this town.   He lost one of his oldest
and best friends, Erwin Rohde, through his hyper-
sensitiveness and lack of the sense of proportion, and
found at last two distinguished readers of his books in
the famous Dane George Brandes, and the French
historian Taine, who wrote to him encouragingly.

The winter of this year was filled out by working
again at the *Will to Power*.   But the work did not pro-
ceed very fast ;   he lacked a definite solution of the
thousand-and-one problems which he had stated.   And his
loneliness weighed on him, he wished for companionship
—perhaps even for marriage.   He knew that if he had

found a noble wife, one like Wagner's Cosima, he would have been happy, more efficient, and saved from the approaching shadows. His health grew worse, he became irritable and more uncritical in his writings.

Whilst in Turin in April 1888 one ray of joy fell into his dreary life. George Brandes wrote him that he was going to deliver a course of lectures on Nietzsche's philosophy. At that time Nietzsche was reading the lawbook of Manu, and, though he liked it, though he placed it high above the Bible, it certainly discouraged him from proceeding with his *Will to Power*. He realised that we do not know enough to construct on such a large scale as he intended to do. And he left his great work, and turned towards the writing of destructive pamphlets.

His Last Books.—Mental disturbance is always preceded by loss of sleep. For years Nietzsche had taken drugs, though at intervals he did without them. Gradually, especially in 1888, the higher brain-centres became slightly disturbed ; yet they could still exercise a considerable influence over the lower and less specialised centres. But the full controlling power of reflection and judgment, such as would prevail were the whole brain at work, was undoubtedly somewhat impaired. In this state he writes to Miss Meysenbug : "I have given the deepest book to Mankind (*Zarathustra*) ; I am the most independent spirit in Europe and the only German writer."

In this state of mind he writes a virulent pamphlet against his former idol and friend, Richard Wagner. The diagnosis of some forms of insanity consists in recording the patient's tendency to false and malevolent assertions concerning people, even his nearest friends. In this pamphlet, *The Case of Wagner*, written in May and June 1888, and published in the autumn, we read that " Wagner is an actor and not a musician ; a symptom of impoverished life, a clever rattlesnake, a typical decadent."

Immediately after this Nietzsche jotted down another

pamphlet, *The Twilight of the Idols*. He spent but
a few days over it, for a feverish haste had come over
him.   At once he sent it to the printer, but it was not
published till after his breakdown. " There is the
waste of an all-too-rich autumn in this book ; you trip
over truths.   You even crush some to death, there are
too many of them.   This treatise is, above all, a recreation, a ray of sunshine, a leap sideways of a psycho-
logist in his leisure moments."   Such was Nietzsche's
opinion about this book, and the alienists tell us that
self-assertion and great hilarity are premonitory mental
symptoms of insanity.   Nietzsche turns out a real
genius for slander ; he goes for everybody, and England, of course, is in for it again : " The English are
the nation of consummate cant—Carlyle, that uncon-
scious and involuntary farce, that heroic moral interpretation of dyspeptic moods.   In England, every man
who indulges in any trifling emancipation from theology
must retrieve his honour in the most terrifying manner
by becoming a moral fanatic. (G. Eliot.)"

Once again, for the last time, Nietzsche turned to his
great work.   He tried new chapter headings, and within
less than a month he composed and compiled what was
to be the first part of the intended great book, and
he called this part *The Antichrist*.   In construction
The Antichrist is decidedly superior to the two preceding books.   Christianity, according to Nietzsche, needs
lies like any other religion, but what stamps Christianity
as the worst and most pernicious of all religions is the
fact that its lies are hostile, dangerous to life.   He calls
Christianity " the one great curse, the one enormous
and innermost perversion, the one great instinct of
revenge."

In September we find Nietzsche in Turin.   For the
first time in ten years one of his books, *The Case of
Wagner*, is noticed by the press.   The complete veering
round of the former Wagnerite is duly recorded by a
few papers.   Nietzsche was in a bright, happy mood
during the last months of 1888 which he spent in Turin.
George Brandes procured him another reader, the

Swede, A. Strindberg. Taine in Paris, Strindberg in Sweden, Brandes in Denmark—the dawn of Nietzsche's fame ! But it was too late. And he seems to have known it. In several letters written by him at that time one can read between the lines the sinister forebodings in his mind.

One more book came from his pen, a kind of autobiography, *Ecce Homo*, a fitting coping-stone to his work before his mental death. Written in a few weeks, it is an interesting document, but sad reading. Self-satisfaction and self-assertion are pushed to the extreme, and a certain incoherence and jumpiness of style are strongly in evidence. The chapter headings are : Why I am so wise ; Why I am so clever ; Why I write such excellent books ; Why I am a fatality. Heine and he are " the greatest artists of the German language that have ever existed " ; " I did a host of things of the highest rank—things that no man can do nowadays." . . . . " To take up one of my books is one of the rarest honours that a man can pay himself " ; . . . " Before my time there was no psychology."

The End.—The catastrophe happened in the beginning of January 1889. Nietzsche went mad. He spoke much and loudly, he paid gold for trifles ; he imagined he was a famous murderer, he was the King of Italy, he was God. He walked about and said to people, " Let us be happy ! I am God, I have made this caricature ! " An old friend of his, Professor Overbeck, fetched the unfortunate man from Turin, and took him into a private institution at Bâle. Then Nietzsche's aged mother came and placed her son in the institution of Dr. Binswanger in Jena, and in 1890 she took him into her house at Naumburg.

What were the causes of Nietzsche's insanity ? We do not know. At any rate not at present, for it is possible that when the medical men who treated Nietzsche publish their data, and when certain other sources of information become accessible, we may know. That the great predisposing cause of an inherited disposition to neurotic disorder may have been there is probable ;

certain, however, it is that there were several exciting causes of insanity at work—overwork, worry, disappointment, and loneliness on the moral side; his accident when a soldier, the illness during the war, his short-sightedness, and drugs on the physical side.

For ten years Nietzsche lingered on. Sometimes there was a slight hope of recovery, but it was not to be. The tragedy of the daring poet-philosopher, who sacrificed his life's health and happiness in order to give mankind a goal and a plan, ends like Tschaïkowsky's "Symphonie Pathétique."

On the 25th August, 1900, Nietzsche died of pneumonia at Weimar, where, after his mother's death, he had been staying with his sister for the last few years. There are a few lines in one of Nietzsche's Dionysus-dithyrambs which seem to be the most fitting epitaph to the life of the creator of the Superman :

> " Amid the warriors
> His was the lightest heart,
> Amid the conquerors
> His brow was dark with thought—
> He was a fate poised on his destiny :
> Unbending, casting thought into the past
> And future, such was he."

CHAPTER II

" BEYOND GOOD AND EVIL "

Principles.—After his breach with Wagner the disillusioned Nietzsche turned from words to facts, from philology towards the study of the exact sciences, especially Physiology. Like a last faithful friend, this science accompanied the lonely scholar to the end. Unfortunately, as he knew and said himself, his knowledge in this and kindred subjects was not deep. Several times he expressed a wish to go for ten years to Paris, Vienna, or Munich, in order to study the natural sciences, but the plan never matured. Yet the wonderful weapons of the classical scholar, combining the armour of Greek culture with the weird power of the poet's winged words, could not fail to do enormous service in the cause of these sciences, and Biology and Eugenics will one day thank that philologist who helped to put down many a prejudice and assisted in clearing the ground for future architects.

On the whole Nietzsche, with Lamarck, believed in adaptation to the environment and the inheritability of acquired characters. Like Spencer, he bases his sociology and ethics on biology, insists upon the elimination of the weak and degenerate. From the biologists Schmidt and Nägeli he took the idea of "mimicry," applying it to ethics; just as many animals, in order not to be seen by their enemies, assume the colour of their environment, so man, through fear of enemies, adopts the moral opinions of the crowd, of his contemporaries. Under the influence of Emerson and the biologists Schneider and Rolph, the idea of environmental influence weakened, and "the Will to Power"—an innate will to grow, to expand, to appropriate—was then considered by Nietzsche to be the chief evolutionary factor. He distinguished between "Masters and Slaves" according to the different *quanta* of energy in different men.

It was due especially to Rolph's influence that Nietzsche adopted the principle of abundance and prosperity as the primary evolutionary principle. Not the competitive fight, the struggle for existence, but the struggle for might, the "Will to Power"! Though with this Nietzsche showed himself an anti-Darwinist and anti-Malthusianist, yet the idea of fight he shared with Darwin. Only in Nietzsche's last period, when the approaching shadows clouded his judgment, did he attack Darwin, as he attacked Lamarck and almost everybody else. Nietzsche considered war and struggle as a biological necessity, as a social necessity. The different parts of our bodies, our different thoughts and sentiments, the members of the same species, all the different species one against another, war, fight, and struggle for pre-eminence, for power.

Definition of Good and Evil.—When Nietzsche used the phrase " Beyond Good and Evil," he did not mean " Beyond Good and Bad." Let us see what he understands by Good and Evil. Good is all that enhances the feeling of power, the Will to Power, and power itself in man. Evil is all that proceeds from weakness, envy, and revenge. How he differentiated between bad and evil and two kinds of good we shall hear later on. Unfortunately he sometimes used these terms indiscriminately.

The worth of all our moral valuations is determined by whether they further or hinder life. All virtues should be looked upon as physiological conditions. Nietzsche goes so far in his biological attitude towards morality that in his autobiography many passages are devoted to the discussion of the importance of properly prepared food.

Morality says, " A race, a people perish through vice and luxury "; Nietzsche says, " When a nation is going to the dogs, when people are degenerating physiologically, vice and luxury (that is to say, the need of ever stronger and more frequent stimuli such as all exhausted natures are acquainted with) are bound to result."

Amorality of the World.—Existence and the world seem justified only as an æsthetic phenomenon ; the world is not good and not bad. Both these terms have significance only with respect to man. There is nothing else on earth but amoral intentions and actions. Nietzsche's leading doctrine about the amorality of the world is : " There are no moral phenomena, there is merely a moral interpretation of phenomena. The origin of this interpretation itself lies beyond the pale of morality."

" All modern moralists after and including Darwin are afraid to establish a moral code of life out of their concepts of Struggle and the privileges of the strong and fit. Like Kant, when it comes to practical morals they construct systems quite independently of the question, What is our conception of the universe ? They are cowards."

Relativism.—Nietzsche was a relativist. Morals, according to him, depend on the geographical and historical conditions of a people. Every conception changes with time. The ancients reckoned envy among the qualities of the good, benevolent goddess Eris. The Greeks likewise differed from us in the value they set upon hope ; they conceived it as blind and deceitful. The Jews, again, took a different view of anger from that which we hold, and sanctified it.

Much that passed for good with one people was regarded with scorn and contempt by another. " Men have given themselves all their good and bad, they took it not, they found it not. Values did man only assign to things in order to maintain himself. Good and evil, which would be everlasting, it doth not exist. All is in flux. Everything good is the evil of yore which has been rendered serviceable."

Nietzsche, who would have rejoiced in Westermarck's great work, *Origin and Development of the Moral Ideas*, wants a " chemistry " of the moral, religious, æsthetic ideas and sentiments—he wants an army of searchers to investigate the origin of such ideas and sentiments. " We need the collection of material, the comprehensive survey and classification of an immense domain of delicate sentiments of worth, and distinctions of worth, which live, grow, propagate, and perish—and perhaps some attempts to give a clear idea of the recurring and more common forms of these living crystallisations— as preparation for a *theory of types* of morality."

Our poet-philosopher, however, had not the patience of the scientist. He did not devote himself to such historical and comparative researches, and compile material for some future master-mind. No, though the material was scanty and his knowledge not thorough —for, after all, biology was only a science read up as far as he was concerned—he set to work both destructively and constructively. He attacked the present moral system and endeavoured to put a better one in its place.

Utilitarian Origin and History of Communal Morality. —Present-day morality is to him a tradition preserving a community, a people. To be moral, correct, and virtuous means to be obedient to an old-established law and custom. The motives of this morality are fear of loss and injury, and hope of usefulness and advantage. Every kind of intimidation has been used to cow all obstreperous individuals. And now where the tradition is old it is almost sacred. To look upon it as a problem, to criticise it, most people consider as immorality itself. All moral valuations are the expression of the needs of a community or herd, of that which is to *its* advantage. By morality the individual is taught to become a function of the herd. As the conditions for the maintenance of one community have been very different from those of another community, there have been very different moralities.

Morality is the herd instinct in the individual. " The pleasure in the herd is older than the pleasure in the ego ; and as long as the good conscience is for the herd, the bad conscience only saith : ego."—Fear is the mother of morals. " The lofty, independent spirituality, the will to stand alone, and even the cogent reason, are felt to be dangers ; everything that elevates the individual above the herd, and is a source of fear to the neighbour, is henceforth called *evil ;* the tolerant, unassuming, self-adapting, self-equalising disposition, the *mediocrity* of desires attains the moral distinction and honour. *Beside* such European herding-morality, *after* it other moralities, higher moralities are or should be possible, especially when the desired stability has been achieved."

Look at the morality of *truthfulness* in the herd. " Thou shalt be recognisable, thou shalt express thy inner nature by means of clear and constant signs— otherwise thou art dangerous. Thou must not remain concealed ; thou must not change ! " Thus, the insistence upon truthfulness has as its main object the recognisability and the stability of the individual,

The just and good man inspires us with the pleasant feelings of security and equality.

" The ' neighbour ' praises unselfishness because *he profits by it !* If the neighbour were ' unselfishly ' disposed himself, he would reject that destruction of power, that injury for *his* advantage, he would thwart such inclinations in their origin, and, above all, he would manifest his unselfishness just by not giving it a good name."

In the *pre-moral period* of mankind the value or non-value of an action was inferred from its *consequences ;* during the *moral period*—the last ten thousand years— " on certain large portions of the earth one no longer lets the consequences. of an action, but its origin, decide with regard to its worth : a great achievement as a whole, an important refinement of vision and of criterion, the first attempt at self-knowledge is thereby made." But with that " an ominous new superstition, a peculiar narrowness of interpretation, attained supremacy. The origin of an action was interpreted in the most definite sense possible, as origin out of an *intention*. People were agreed in the belief that the value of an action lay in the value of its intention."

" Is it not possible that we may be standing on the threshold of a period which to begin with, would be distinguished negatively as *ultra-moral :* nowadays, when, at least amongst us immoralists, the suspicion arises that the decisive value of an action lies precisely in that which is *not intentional*, and that all its intentionalness, all that is seen, sensible, or ' sensed ' in it, belongs to its surface or skin—which, like every skin, betrays something, but *conceals* still more ? In short, we believe that morality, in the sense in which it has been understood hitherto, as *intention*-morality, has been a prejudice, perhaps a prematureness or preliminariness, probably something of the same rank as astrology and alchemy, but in any case something which must be surmounted."

Compulsion precedes morality, indeed, morality itself is compulsion for a time, to which one submits for the

avoidance of pain.   Later on it becomes custom—later
still, free obedience, and, finally, almost instinct—
then, like everything long-accustomed and natural, it
is connected with pleasure—and is henceforth called
virtue.   Since, however, no one is really responsible for
his action, the concept of free will being a happy de-
lusion, remorse is cowardice.   What is the good of it
all in the end !   No deed gets undone because it is
regretted, no more than because it is "forgiven" or
"expiated."   Formerly people argued : Conscience condemns this action, therefore this action is reprehensible.
But, as a matter of fact, conscience condemns an action
because that action has been condemned by custom for a
long period of time : all conscience does is to imitate : it
does not create values; that which first led to the con-
demnation of certain actions was *not* conscience : but the
knowledge of or the prejudice against their consequence,
the approbation of conscience, the feeling of well-being,
of "inner peace," is of the same order of emotions as
the artist's joy over his work—it proves nothing.   "We
are far too ignorant to be able to judge of the value of
our actions."

"Sinfulness" in man is not an actual fact, but
rather merely the interpretation of a fact, of a physiological discomfort.   The fact, therefore, that any one
feels "guilty," "sinful," is certainly not yet any proof
that he is right in feeling so, any more than one is healthy
simply because he feels healthy.   "Remember the cele-
brated witch-ordeals : in those days the most acute
and humane judges had no doubt but that in these
cases they were confronted with guilt—the ' witches '
themselves had no doubt on the point—and yet the guilt
was lacking."

But though Nietzsche thus attacks the moral conscience, he regrets the lack of the intellectual conscience
in most men.   "They continue to make use of their
scales, calling this good and that bad ; and they do not
blush for shame when one remarks that these weights
are not the full amount.   Most people do not find it
contemptible to believe this or that, and live according

to it without having been previously aware of the ultimate and surest reason for and against it, and without even giving themselves any trouble about such reasons afterwards. To stand in the midst of this tangle, this sorry scheme of things, harmonious and discordant at the same time, to stand in the midst of all the marvellous uncertainty and ambiguity of existence, *and not to question*, not to tremble with desire and delight in questioning, not even to hate the questioner—perhaps even to make merry over him to the extent of weariness —that is what I regard as *contemptible*."

Free Will.—This delightful onslaught of Nietzsche is quite comprehensible in view of the modern indolence and indifference, but it loses its foundation if we consider that he denied the existence of a free will. According to him nobody is responsible for his actions, nobody for his nature ; to judge is identical with being unjust. This also applies when an individual judges himself. " We do not complain of nature as immoral because it sends a thunderstorm and makes us wet,—why do we call those who injure us immoral ? Because in the latter case we take for granted a free will functioning voluntarily ; in the former we see necessity. But this distinction is an error." We kill the fly, the criminal. All systems of morals allow intentional injury in the case of necessity—that is, when it is a matter of self-preservation. Yet the fly, the criminal did well—that is, they did that which seemed to them good (useful) according to the degree of their intellect.

" Furthermore, our ordinary inaccurate observation takes a group of phenomena as one, and calls them a fact. Between this fact and another we imagine a vacuum, we isolate each fact. In reality, however, the sum of our actions and cognitions is no series of facts and intervening vacua, but a continuous stream." Its sources are hidden away in the dim past (heredity) and the mystery of the present (environment). Now, the belief in free will is " incompatible with the idea of a continuous, uniform, undivided, indivisible flow ; this belief presupposes that every single action is isolated and indivisible ; it is an atomic theory as regards volition and cognition." Owing to the rigidity and many other shortcomings of our language we are constantly induced to think of things as simpler than they really are. " Language is the continual apostle and advocate of the belief in free will."

Behind all logic there are valuations, or, to speak more plainly, physiological demands, for the maintenance of a definite mode of life. Besides, man is an *individuum*, and in ethics he will consider himself as a *dividuum*. A man who *wills* commands *something* within himself which renders obedience, or which he believes renders obedience. Freedom of will is " the expression for the complex state of delight of the person exercising this volition. The person exercising volition adds the feelings of delight in his successful executive instruments, the useful ' under-wills ' or ' under-souls '—indeed, our body is but a social structure composed of many souls—to his feelings of delight as commander. What happens here is what happens in every well-constructed and happy commonwealth— namely, that the governing class identifies itself with the successes of the commonwealth." The unknown physiological factors which we label with the synthetic word Ego are the governing class.

" It is the extravagant pride of man, this desire for freedom of will, this desire to bear the entire and ultimate responsibility for one's actions oneself and to absolve God, the world, ancestors, chance, and society therefrom ; it is the most egregious theological trick that has ever existed for the purpose of making mankind ' responsible ' in a theological manner—that is to say, to make mankind dependent upon theologians.

" No one is responsible for the fact that he exists at all, that he is constituted as he is, and that he happens to be in certain circumstances and in a particular environment. The fatality of his being cannot be divorced from the fatality of all that which has been and will be."

Pity.—Free will was one of Nietzsche's bugbears.

Pity, however, fares worse at his hands. He, the biologist-philosopher, thought to find in pity the greatest impediment to a full development of life. Pity is a waste of feeling, a moral parasite which is injurious to health. Pity does not depend upon maxims, but upon emotions. The suffering we see infects us ; pity is an infection.

" Pity is opposed to the tonic passions which enhance the energy of the feeling of life, its action is depressing. A man loses power when he pities. On the whole, pity thwarts the law of development which is the law of selection. It preserves that which is ripe for death, it fights in favour of the disinherited and the condemned of life. By multiplying misery quite as much as by preserving all that is miserable, it is the principal agent in promoting decadence."

Cowardice and weakness are often the causes of pity. " The greatest of almsgivers is cowardice. All those who are not sufficiently masters of themselves and do not regard morality as a self-control and self-conquest continuously exercised in things great and small, unconsciously come to glorify the good, compassionate, benevolent impulses of that instinctive morality which has no head, but seems merely to consist of a heart and helpful hands."

Christianity is called the religion of pity. " The most general effect, the most complete transformation that Christianity has produced in Europe is perhaps the fact that the man who performs social, sympathetic, disinterested, and benevolent actions is now considered as *the* moral man. Christianity itself when flourishing was thoroughly selfish, for the Christian cared really but for the one thing needful, the absolute importance of eternal and *personal* salvation. Now where Christian dogmas are gradually receding, where people become gradually separated from these dogmas, there they seek the more some sort of justification for this separation in a cult of the love of humanity." Since the French Revolution, a John Stuart Mill in England, a Schopenhauer in Germany, and the socialists everywhere have brought into the greatest prominence this doctrine of sympathetic affections and of pity or utility to others as a principle of action. And they all are sure that that is morality. " But the trouble is that at the present time there is perhaps no more widely spread prejudice than that of thinking that we know what really and truly constitutes morality." Nietzsche, the biological fanatic and idealist, deals finally a death-stroke to pity and sympathy with these words : " The weak and the botched shall perish ; first principle of our humanity. And they ought even to be helped to perish. What is more harmful than any vice ? Practical sympathy with all the botched and the weak— Christianity ! "

" **Will to Power.**"—So far Nietzsche the destructive moralist. Let us now hear him as to what is his constructive policy. Two ideas permeate this policy— " Will to Power " and " Master and Slave Morality." The motive power of all organic life, according to Nietzsche, is not the " Will to Live," which he thinks nonsense, but the desire to expand, to grow, to appropriate, to gain in power—in short, the " Will to Power." And with respect to the second concept, " Master and Slaves," one must never lose sight of the fact that Nietzsche's philosophy to a certain extent is an esoteric philosophy, a class-philosophy intended for the elect, for " higher men," for the aristocracy of intellect. At any rate, so his disciples assure us. All his destructive views and methods of attack on present-day morality are only for the elect, the " masters " ; the masses, the " slaves," the herd, need the present-day morality, and one must not take from them this morality which supplies them with " the pillars of their existence and the soporific appliances towards happiness." And again, all his constructive views and hints cannot be taken up without danger by any one but the " masters."

" Wherever I found a living thing, there found I the Will to Power ; and even in the will of the servant found I the will to be master. Neither necessity nor desire, but the love of power, is the demon of mankind. You may give men everything possible—health, food, shelter, enjoyment—but they are and remain unhappy and capricious, for the demon waits and waits and must be satisfied."

" Passion for power is the earthquake which breaketh and upbreaketh all that is rotten and hollow ; the rolling, rumbling, punitive demolisher of whited sepulchres ; the flashing interrogative sign besides premature answers ; passion for power : before whose glance man creepeth and croucheth and drudgeth, and becometh lower than the serpent and the swine, until at last great contempt crieth out of him."

" The criterion of truth lies in the enhancement of the feeling of power." With this statement, which, like so many others, shows the pragmatic tendency of some parts of his philosophy, Nietzsche attacks Spencer, who makes constraint or inability the criterion of truth when he says : " The unconceivableness of its negation is the ultimate test of the truth of a proposition." And the pragmatists say : " Theories are only tools, the value of which lies in their power to work." These theories, by leading up to new truths and to suitable conduct, by influencing our knowledge and our life purposively by all this, these theories are pragmatically " true "— *i.e.* good, valuable, useful, furthering life. Truth is that which furthers us on the way of thinking, which leads us from one experience to another, which proves to be good intellectually, which is the best leader, which suits best every part of life, which agrees best with the totality of our experiences. Now the delight man derives from his power to work, especially an increased power to work, from the feeling of being furthered, led, is certainly similar to that which Nietzsche calls " Will to Power." Says Peirce, the founder of Pragmatism : " The entire intellectual purport of any symbol consists in the total of all general modes of rational conduct which, conditionally upon all the possible different circumstances and desires, would ensue upon the acceptance." Putting aside for the moment their artistic " purport," if we do not find a certain similar

" intellectual purport " in Nietzsche's symbols of " Will
to Power," " Superman," why go on ?

Similar views we find in other statements of Nietzsche.
It is our needs that interpret the world, our instincts
and their impulses for and against. Every instinct is
a sort of thirst for power ; each has its point of view,
which it would fain impose upon all the other instincts
as their norm. Even in our very bodies there is a
fight for power between the cells and the tissues.

" Man does not seek happiness and does not avoid
unhappiness. Everybody knows the famous prejudices
hereby contradicted. Pleasure and pain are mere
results, mere accompanying phenomena ; that which
every man, which every tiny particle of a living organism
will have, is an increase in power. In striving after this,
pleasure and pain are encountered. Pain as the hin-
drance of the organism's will to power is therefore a
normal feature, a natural ingredient of every organic
phenomenon ; man does not avoid it—on the contrary, he is constantly in need of it. Every triumph,
every feeling of pleasure, every event presupposes an
obstacle overcome."

Morality of " Masters and Slaves."—" In a tour
through the many finer and coarser moralities which
have hitherto prevailed or still prevail on the earth,
certain traits can be found recurring regularly together
and connected with one another, until finally two
primary types reveal themselves, and a radical distinction is brought to light. There is master-morality
and slave-morality. Of course in all higher and mixed
civilisations there are also attempts at the reconciliation
of the two moralities."

Guided by this concept of master and slave morality,
Nietzsche proceeds to give us another cause and origin
of the differentiation between good and its opposite,
an origin in its *general* application much at variance, or
at any rate not quite in harmony, with that he gives
when he speaks of morality as a tradition and custom
preserving a community, a people. The ideas of
security, usefulness, and advantage which are the

motive powers in such a communal morality-preserving custom are more and more discarded. The "Will to Power" takes their place.

According to Nietzsche, the distinctions of moral values have either originated in a ruling caste, the masters, pleasantly conscious of being different from the ruled, or among the ruled class, the slaves and dependents of all sorts. The antithesis "good" and "bad" amongst the masters means practically the same as "noble" and "despicable"; the antithesis "good" and "evil" amongst the slaves means "useful" and "dangerous." Slave morality is essentially the morality of utility. "The ignoble nature is distinguished by the fact that it keeps its advantage steadily in view, and that this thought of the end and advantage is even stronger than its strongest impulses, not to be tempted to inexpedient activities by its impulses—that is, its wisdom and inspiration. In comparison with this ignoble nature the higher nature is more irrational."

The problem of the "good"—as these resentful slaves have thought it out—demands its solution. "It is not surprising that the lambs should bear a grudge against the great birds of prey, but that is no reason for blaming the great birds of prey for taking the little lambs. And when the lambs say among themselves, 'These birds of prey are evil, and he who is so far removed from being a bird of prey, who is rather its opposite, a lamb, is he not good?' Then there is nothing to cavil at in the setting up of this ideal, though it may also be that the birds of prey will regard it a little sneeringly, and perchance say to themselves, '*We* bear no grudge against them, these good lambs, we even like them : nothing is tastier than a tender lamb.'"

The solution Nietzsche proposes is one which will not endear him to the democrat. Of course there is to be considered the fact that Nietzsche led a sheltered life like many of our dons and professors ; real want, real misery as a Dostoievsky knew it, he never saw and felt. So it is to be explained that he who was after all but an amateur in the handling of the vast and complex problems of political economy *sometimes* makes one smile. He considers the democratic movement not only as a degenerating form of political organisation, but democrats as equivalent to a degenerating, a waning type of man, as involving his mediocrising and depreciation.

"Men are not equal." And the solution is that we *must* have the two classes, masters and men. "A higher culture can only originate where there are two distinct castes of society, that of the working class, and that of the leisured class who are capable of true leisure ; or, more strongly expressed, the caste of compulsory labour and the caste of free labour. Slavery is of the essence of Culture."

But where Nietzsche's esoteric philosophy aims at inculcating new virtues in his master-class he is wonderful, and certainly, even to the masses he does not like, many of his precepts ought to be ideals ; and at any rate his tenets are powerful antidotes to some of the present-day shallowness and senseless equalisation. Here, in his commandments to the masters, the " higher men," Nietzsche's " Beyond-Good-and-Evil Morality " is decidedly constructive.

" One must learn to love oneself with a wholesome and healthy love, that one may endure to be with oneself and not go roving about. O my brethren, a new nobility is needed, which shall be the adversary of all populace and potentate rule, and shall inscribe anew the word ' noble ' on new tables. And *what is noble ? To be able to command and to obey !* Severe and genuine culture should consist above all in obedience and habituation." Nietzsche hates the anarchists because they undermine such a culture.

Master morality has " profound reverence for age and for tradition. Here we find utility and obligation to exercise prolonged gratitude and prolonged revenge— both only within the circle of equals—artfulness in retaliation. Signs of nobility : never to think of lowering our duties to the rank of duties for everybody ;

to be unwilling to renounce or to share our responsibilities ; to count our prerogatives, and the exercise of them, among our duties."

Nietzsche tries to justify his differentiating between master and slave morality by etymology, a procedure quite worthy of a philologist. The whole of the first essay in his book, *The Genealogy of Morals*, deals with the problem, and is entitled " Good and Evil, Good and Bad." The reader who wants to go deeper into the question must be specially referred to this book. There he will find Nietzsche's wish that some faculty of philosophy should consider the following question for a prize essay : " What indication of the history of the evolution of the moral ideas is afforded by philology, and especially by etymological investigation ? "

He says it is obvious that everywhere the designations of moral value were at first applied to *men*, and were only derivatively and at a later period applied to *actions*. " What is the true etymological significance of the various symbols for the idea ' good ' which have been coined in the various languages ? They all lead back to the same evolution of the same idea—that everywhere ' aristocrat,' ' noble ' (in the social sense) is the root idea." Nietzsche's intimate acquaintance with the Greek thinker Theognis probably gave him the first clue. The Greek adjective ἀγαθός, good, means brave, skilful, able ; κακός, bad, means vulgar, plebeian, cowardly. The Latin *bonus*, good, means the warrior (?), and *malus*, bad, he places side by side with the Greek μέλας, black, because the vulgar men in the early Roman days could be distinguished by the dark colour of their skin and above all by their black hair as the pre-Aryan inhabitants of the Italian soil. Gaelic has afforded the exact analogue —*Fin* (for instance, in the name Fin-Gal), the distinctive word of the nobility, finally—good, noble, clean, but originally the blond-haired man in contrast to the dark, black-haired aboriginals. The German word, " *schlicht*," simple, became " *schlecht*," bad.—Nietzsche might have quoted the Greek word signifying wickedness (πονηρία) which comes from the word signifying labour (πόνος) : a truly aristocratic attitude !

So far the influence of value-creating " masters " on the language. On the other hand, " everywhere that *slave-morality* gains the ascendency, language *shows a tendency to approximate the significations of the words ' good ' and ' stupid.* ' "—Nietzsche might have quoted here our " *silly*," which is the Old English " *saelig* " or blessed ; our word " *simple*," originally applying to one " of a single fold," a Nathanael, whom as such Christ honoured to the highest (John i. 47). Now we call an idiot or one otherwise deficient in intellect an " *innocent*," or one who does not hurt. The German word " *albern*," simple, once meant quite true, friendly. *Sic transit gloria virtutis !*

Future Morality.—What does Nietzsche imagine the future morality, *i.e.* the morality of future masters, to be like ? Compared with the present generation, the future one " will seem more evil—for in good as in evil they will be more *straightforward*. They will do the good for its own sake, not like the present slaves, who want to be paid for their virtues by future bliss."— " We ought to have the courage to become conscious, and to affirm all that which has been attained—to get rid of the humdrum character of old valuations, which makes us unworthy of the best and strongest things that we have achieved. An order of rank will be established, based upon real values. There will be no remorse in man's heart any longer. Those healthy men of the future will laugh at the seriousness and ardour with which we allowed ourselves to be hypnotised to any extent by any detail in our lives, and our remorse will seem to them like the action of a dog biting a stone. They will hate to leave an action of theirs in the lurch.

As heretofore, all progress in morals has been made by means of crime, since the days when Prometheus stole the fire from the gods ; thus this future morality will not be reached without violent revolutions, without crime. The best and highest that men can acquire they obtain by crime. Everyone who has hitherto overthrown a law of established morality has always at first been considered as a *wicked man :* but when it was afterwards found impossible to re-establish the law, and people gradually became accustomed to the change, the epithet was changed by slow degrees. History deals almost exclusively with these " *wicked men,* who later on came to be recognised as *good men.* The changes and transformations which hitherto have taken place in morals were caused by successful crimes. All good things were once bad things ; from every original sin has grown an original virtue. Marriage, for example, seemed for a long time a sin against the rights of the community ; a man formerly paid a fine for the insolence of claiming one woman to himself."

War.—However, that which will distinguish most clearly the future men who will live according to Nietzsche's code of morals is their courage, their fearlessness, their love of war. They will fight men, gods, and stars. Says Nietzsche : " If ye cannot be saints of knowledge, then, I pray you, be at least its warriors. War and courage have done more great things than charity. What is the good ? ye ask. To be brave is good. Live your life of obedience and of war ! Let your love to life be love to your highest hope ; and let your highest hope be the highest thought of life ! "

" Nothing separates the Greek world more from ours than the idea of contest, of fight. The Greek is envious, and conceives of this quality not as a blemish but as the effect of a beneficent deity. Every natural gift must develop itself by contest. Thus the Hellenic national pedagogy demands. One will have to pardon my occasionally chanting a pæan of war. Horribly clangs its silvery bow ; and, although it comes along like the night, war is nevertheless Apollo, the true divinity for consecrating and purifying the State.

" For nations that are growing weak and contemptible, war may be prescribed as a remedy, if indeed they really want to go on living. National consumption, as well as individual, admits of a brutal cure. The eternal will to live and inability to die is, however, in itself already a sign of senility of emotion. The more fully and thoroughly we live, the more ready we are to sacrifice life for a single pleasurable emotion. A people that lives and feels in this wise has no need of war."

Nietzsche's ideas about war may seem reactionary to the reader, and probably they are reactionary, and they certainly will shock all pacifists, but we must not forget that growing and powerful nations still adhere nowadays to similar views. The tremendous, almost insane, preparations of all the Great Powers at the present time are a symptom.

If the reader wants to become acquainted with some of the causes of this disease, or, as Nietzsche would say, of this virtue, let him read the book *Germany and the Next War*, by Bernhardi, a German general. There we read : " *War is a biological necessity,* an indispensable regulator in the life of mankind, failing which would result a course of evolution deleterious to the species and, too, utterly antagonistic to all culture. War, said Heraclitus, is the father of all things. Without war, inferior or demoralised races would only too easily swamp the healthy and vital ones, and a general decadence would be the consequence. War is one of the essential factors of morality. If circumstances require, it is not only the right but the moral and political duty of a statesman to bring about a war ! " This book, which bears on its title-page as a motto Nietzsche's words : " War and courage have done more great things than the love to the neighbour," was published only this year, and has run into several editions.

After that we close with a sigh Norman Angell's book, *The Great Illusion.* And we give up in despair— at any rate for the present—this hope of Angell's that international economic interests and enlightened public opinion will prevent war. And who will deny that there is some truth in Nietzsche's words when he says, " I cannot help seeing in the prevailing international movements of the present day, and the simultaneous promulgation of universal suffrage, the effects of the fear of war above everything else—yea, I behold behind these movements those truly international homeless money-hermits, as the really alarmed, who, with their natural lack of the State-ideal, have learnt to abuse politics as a means of the exchange, and State and Society as an apparatus for their own enrichment. Against the deviation of the State-ideal into a Money-ideal, to be feared from this side, *the only remedy is war, and once again war,* in the emotions of which this at least becomes obvious, that the State is not founded upon the fear of the war demon as a protective institution for egoistic individuals, but that *in love to father-land and prince it produces an ethical impulse indicative of a much higher destiny !* "

CHAPTER III

THE ANTICHRIST

Principles.—Nietzsche's great masters, the Greek philosophers Heraclitus and Empedocles, have anticipated several modern ideas, the former that of Evolution, the latter Darwin's idea of Natural Selection. Our philosopher was even fond of calling Darwin's idea a special application of the fundamental idea of Empedocles. Unfortunately Nietzsche, like so many others, did not distinguish clearly between Evolution and Natural Selection. He perceived, however, that the value of the theory of Natural Selection lies in its idea of elimination.

With Spencer he observed that there is a serious lack of elimination amongst men, since it is hindered by several counteracting factors. He believed the worst impediment to elimination was and still is the Christian Church, because the latter protects and preserves the unfit and weak. Next to it, again like Spencer, he places Pity, because it only palliates momentary suffer-

ings and persists in overlooking the infinitely vaster
indirect evils which it produces by its shortsighted
policy.

Christianity *v.* Selection.—" The attacks made upon
Christianity hitherto have been not only timid but
false. So long as Christian morality was not felt to be
a *capital crime against Life* its apologists had a good
time. The question concerning the mere ' truth ' of
Christianity—whether in regard to the existence of its
God or to the legendary history of its origin, not to
speak of its astronomy and natural science—is quite
beside the point as long as no inquiry is made into the
value of Christian *morality*. Are Christian morals
worth anything, or are they a profanation and an out-
rage, despite all the arts of holiness and seduction with
which they are enforced ? The question concerning
the truth of the religion may be met by all sorts of
subterfuges ; and the most fervent believers can, in
the end, avail themselves of the logic used by their
opponents, in order to create a right for their side to
assert that certain things are irrefutable—that is to
say, they *transcend* the means employed to refute them.
(Nowadays this trick of dialectics is called ' Kantian
Criticism ') . . . ."

" *Christianity is the reverse of the principle of selection.*
If the degenerate and sick man (' the Christian ') is to
be of the same value as the healthy man (' the pagan '),
the natural course of evolution is thwarted and the
unnatural becomes law. What the species requires is
the suppression of the physiologically botched, the
weak, and the degenerate ; but it was precisely to these
people that Christianity appealed as a preservative
force. It simply strengthened that natural and very
strong instinct of all the weak which bids them protect,
maintain, and mutually support each other. Christian
altruism is the mob-egotism of the weak. He who does
not consider this attitude of mind as immoral, as a
crime against life, belongs himself to the sickly crowd,
and also shares their instincts. Genuine love of mankind exacts sacrifice for the good of the species ; it is

hard, full of self-control, because it needs human sacrifice."

Christianity is an artful device, consciously and sub-consciously evolved for the self-preservation and advantage of the inferior classes of society; it is a kind of Salvation Army movement of long standing. " Does it not actually seem that some single will has ruled over Europe for eighteen centuries in order to make a sublime abortion of men ? Christianity has waged a deadly war upon the *higher* type of man, it has set a ban upon all the fundamental instincts of this type, and has distilled evil and the devil himself out of these instincts. Christianity has sided with everything weak, low, and botched ; it has made an ideal out of *antagonism* against all the self-preservative instincts of strong life ; it has corrupted the reason of the strongest intellects, by teaching that the highest values of intellectuality are sinful, misleading, and full of temptations."

According to Nietzsche all religions are pious false-hoods. In his masterly essay on " Truth and Falsity " and in many other passages, he points out that at present falsehoods, illusions, are often more valuable to man, more life-preserving, than truth. But he attacks Christianity because the lies of the Bible are unlike those of the venerable lawbook of Manu. The latter epitomises the experience, the precautionary measures, and the experimental morality of long ages ; " all those things which Christianity smothers with its bottom-less vulgarity—procreation, woman, marriage—are here treated with earnestness, with reverence, with love and confidence ; its illusions are the means by which the noble classes, the philosophers and the warriors, guard and guide the masses. But in the Bible such ends holy to Life are entirely absent ; its illusions aim at bad ends—the poisoning, the calumniation and the denial of life, the contempt of the body, the degradation and self-pollution of man by virtue of the concept sin. *In point of fact, it matters greatly to what end one lies, whether one preserves or destroys by means of falsehood.* It is quite justifiable to bracket the Christian and the Anarchist together ; their object, their instinct, is concerned only with destruction."

Origin of Christianity.—Each religion has been born of fear and necessity. Often it has been a sort of fear and sensation of terror in one's own presence. But the Christian religion is essentially a product of the slave-class ; the slaves feared their masters, the slaves wanted power too, the slaves were in the majority and they won the day. Christianity was the revolt of the physiologically inferior people. It is a typical form of decadence, of moral softening and of hysteria, " amidst a general hotch-potch of races and peoples that had lost all aims and had grown weary and sick." It is the transvaluation of all Aryan values, the triumph of Chandala values, the general insurrection of all the downtrodden and wretched against the race.

The Oriental element in Christianity predominates. " It knows it is a matter of indifference whether a thing be true or not, but that it is of the highest importance that it should be believed to be true." Again, we find an Oriental element in this : " In order that the lowest instincts may also make their voices heard, God must be young. For the ardour of the women a beautiful saint, and for the ardour of the men a Virgin Mary, has to be pressed into the foreground." Further, consider this thought : " ' Whom the Lord loveth, He chasteneth.' Women in the Orient hold castigations and the strict seclusion of their persons from the world to be signs of their husband's love." Christianity is full of hysteria.

" That strange and morbid world into which the gospels lead us—a world which seems to have been drawn from a Russian novel, where the scum and dross of society, diseases of the nerves and ' childish ' imbecility, seem to have given each other rendezvous, would have been the proper material for the pen of a Dostoievsky. All those holy epileptics and visionaries did not possess a thousandth part of the honesty in self-criticism with which a philologist nowadays reads a text or tests the truth of an historical event."

Eternal Life.—" That everybody as an ' immortal soul ' should have equal rank, that in the totality of beings the ' salvation ' of each individual may lay claim to eternal importance, that insignificant bigots and three-quarter-lunatics may have the right to suppose that the laws of nature may be persistently broken on their account—any such magnification of every kind of selfishness to infinity, to insolence, cannot be branded with sufficient contempt. And yet it is to this miserable flattery of personal vanity that Christianity owes its triumph ; by this means it lured all the bungled and the botched, all revolting and revolted people, all abortions, the whole of the refuse and offal of humanity, over to its side. The ' salvation of the soul '—in plain English, the world revolves around me."

Sin.—" The notions of guilt and punishment, including the doctrines of ' grace,' of ' salvation,' and of ' forgiveness '—all *lies* through and through, without a shred of psychological reality—were invented in order to destroy man's sense of causality ; they were an attack on the concept of cause and effect ! And not an attack with the fist, the knife, with honesty in hate and love, but one actuated by the most cowardly, most crafty, and most ignoble instincts. A priest's attack ! A parasite's attack ! A vampyrism of pale subterranean leeches ! When the natural consequences of an act are no longer ' natural,' but are thought to be conjured up by phantom concepts of superstition, by ' God,' by ' spirits,' and by ' souls,' as merely moral consequences, in the form of rewards, punishments, hints, and educational means, then the whole basis of knowledge is destroyed, then the greatest crime against man has been perpetrated. Sin, I repeat, this form of self-pollution *par excellence* on the part of man, was invented in order to make science, culture, and every elevation and noble trait in man quite impossible ; by means of the invention of sin the priest is able to *rule*."

Historical Results of Christianity.—" The whole labour of the ancient world in vain ! I am at a loss for a word which could express my feelings at something so atrocious. All the prerequisites of learned culture, all the scientific methods already existed; the great and peerless art of reading well had already been established; natural science, hand in hand with mathematics and mechanics, was on the best possible road; the sense for facts, the last and most valuable of all senses, had its schools and its tradition, was already centuries old! Everything *essential* had been discovered to make it possible for work to be begun— methods; and, this cannot be said too often, they are the essential thing, also the most difficult thing, while they moreover have to wage the longest war against custom and indolence. That which to-day we have successfully reconquered for ourselves, by dint of unspeakable self-discipline, the impartial eye for reality, the cautious hand, patience and seriousness in the smallest details, complete uprightness in knowledge— all this was already there; it had been there over two thousand years before! All this in vain! In one night it became merely a memory! The Greeks! The Romans! Instinctive nobility, instinctive taste, methodic research, the genius of organisation and administration, faith, the *will* to the future of mankind, the great yea to all things, materialised in the Imperium Romanum, become visible to all the senses, grand style no longer manifested in mere art, but in reality, in truth, in *life!* And buried in a night, not by a natural catastrophe! Not stamped to death by Teutons and other heavy-footed Vandals! But destroyed by crafty, stealthy, invisible anæmic vampires! Not conquered, but only drained of blood!

" Everything wretched, inwardly ailing, and full of ignoble feelings, the whole Ghetto-world of souls, was in a trice *uppermost!* One only needs to read any one of the Christian agitators—St. Augustine, for instance—in order to realise, in order to *smell,* what filthy fellows came to the top in this movement."—

Christianity destroyed the harvest we might have reaped from the culture of antiquity; later it also destroyed our harvest of the culture of Islam. The wonderful Moorish world of Spanish culture was trampled to death! "Later on the Crusaders waged war on something before which it would have been more seemly in them to grovel in the dust. Crusades! Superior piracy, that is all!"

St. Paul.—Nietzsche was very indulgent towards Christ. He rarely hurls his invectives against the "founder of a little Jewish sect." All his hatred of Christianity is poured out on St. Paul, whom he holds responsible for Christianity, whom he considers the founder of it. "St. Paul was one of the most ambitious and importunate souls that ever existed, of a mind full of superstition and cunning. That the ship of Christianity threw overboard no inconsiderable part of its Jewish ballast, that it was able to sail into the waters of the heathen and actually did do so, this is due to the history of this one single man.

"St. Paul was a slave-mind who revolted against the Law. As he suggests here and there, he had many things on his conscience—hatred, murder, sorcery, idolatry, debauchery, drunkenness, and orgiastic revelry —and to however great an extent he tried to soothe his conscience, and even more, his desire for power, by the extreme fanaticism of his worship for and defence of the Law, there were times when the thought struck him: 'It is all in vain!' And at last a liberating thought, together with a vision—which was only to be expected in the case of an epileptic like himself— flashed into his mind: to him, the stern upholder of the Law—who, in his innermost heart, was tired to death of it—there appeared on the lonely path that Christ, with the divine effulgence on His countenance, and Paul heard the words: 'Why persecutest thou Me?'

"What actually took place, then, was this: his mind was suddenly enlightened, and he said to himself, Here is my means of escape, here is my complete vengeance, here and nowhere else have I the destroyer of the Law in my hands! From that time forward he would be the apostle of the annihilation of the Law;

He became the first Christian, the inventor of Christianity ! Before him there were only a few Jewish sectaries.

" The ' gospel ' died on the cross. That which thenceforward was called ' gospel ' was the reverse of that ' gospel ' that Christ had lived : it was ' evil tidings,' a dysangel.

" It is false to the point of nonsense to see in ' faith,' in the faith in salvation through Christ, the distinguishing trait of the Christian : the only thing that is Christian is the Christian mode of existence, a life such as he led who died on the cross. To this day a life of this kind is still possible. *Not* a faith, but a course of action, above all a course of inaction, non-interference. You now realise what it was that came to an end with the death on the cross—a new and thoroughly original effort towards a Buddhistic movement of peace, towards *real* and not merely *promised* happiness on earth.

" Paul appeared with his bad conscience and his thirst for power. He forged and distorted the life, doctrine, and death of the ' Saviour ' ; he falsified the history of Israel, so as to make it appear as a prologue to *his* mission : all the prophets had referred to *his* ' Saviour.' What he himself did not believe was believed in by the idiots among whom he spread *his* doctrine." He bribed Christ's disciples and followers, who felt resentment against dominant Judaism, the ruling class, the Pharisees, and theologians—Paul bribed these " completely unhinged souls, who felt themselves in revolt against established order, by the most contemptible of all unrealisable promises, the impudent doctrine of personal immortality and those products of resentment, *Our* God, the *Only* God, and the *Only* Son of God. The Christian is nothing more than an anarchical Jew. And Paul, this appalling impostor, pandered to the instincts of Chandala morality in those paltry people when he said : ' *Not many noble are called.* But God hath chosen the foolish things of the world to confound the wise . . . and base things of the world ' (1 Cor. i. 20 *et seq.*)."

Christianity *v.* **Human Love.**—Nietzsche knows no words strong enough to fit his anger. " Christianity has succeeded in transforming Eros and Aphrodite— sublime powers, capable of idealisation—into hellish genii and phantom goblins, by means of the pangs which every sexual impulse was made to raise in the conscience of the believers. And the outcome of this diabolisation of Eros is a mere farce since the ' demon ' Eros has become an object of greater interest to mankind than all the angels and saints put together, thanks to the mysterious Mumbo-Jumboism of the Church in all things erotic : it is due to the Church that love stories, even in our time, have become the one common interest which appeals to all classes of people—with an exaggeration which would be incomprehensible to antiquity, and which will not fail to provoke roars of laughter in coming generations."

Christianity *v.* **Art.**—Nietzsche, who in his *Birth of Tragedy* defended a purely æsthetic world-interpretation, sees no greater antithesis to his tenet than the Christian dogma, " which is only and will be only moral, and which, with its absolute standards, for instance, its truthfulness of God, relegates—that is disowns, convicts, condemns art, *all* art, to the realm of falsehood " ; to him this religion which " thinks the last hour of a man's life the most important, that has prophesied the end of earthly life and condemned all creatures to live in the fifth act of a tragedy, is an enemy to all new planting, to all bold attempts or free aspirations " ; to him " faith does not prove anything " —" a mere casual stroll through a lunatic asylum will make that clear—and martyrs do not do so either— even to this day it only requires the crude fact of persecution in order to create an honourable name for an obscure sect which does not matter in the least " ; to him, though Christianity has now developed into a " soft moralism, it is no longer a matter of reason but of taste that decides against Christianity."

GOD.—The attitude Nietzsche assumes towards the concept of God is, if that is possible, still more uncompromising than that which he takes up towards the Christian Church. On the whole, however, he attacks the god-idea of the Christians only. The reader is probably acquainted with the lines in the *Rubáiyát*, where Omar Khayyám listens to the Earthen Lot in that old Potter's Shop :

> " Then said another—' Surely not in vain
> My substance from the common Earth was ta'en,
> That He who subtly wrought me into Shape
> Should stamp me back to common Earth again.'
>
> Another said—' Why, ne'er a peevish Boy
> Would break the Bowl from which he drank in Joy;
> Shall He that made the Vessel in pure Love
> And Fancy, in an after Rage destroy ! ' "

Says the iconoclast Nietzsche : " Too much miscarried with him, this potter who has not learned thoroughly ! That he took revenge on his pots and creations, however, because they turned out badly—that was a sin against *good taste*.

" He was a hidden God, full of secrecy. Verily, he did not come by his son otherwise than by secret ways. At the door of his faith standeth adultery. When he was young, that God out of the Orient, then he was harsh and revengeful and built himself a hell for the delight of his favourites. At last, however, he became old and soft and mellow and pitiful, more like a grandfather than a father, but most like a tottering old grandmother. There did he sit shrivelled in his chimney-corner, fretting on account of his weak legs, world-weary, will-weary, and one day he suffocated of his all-too-great pity.

" An omniscient and omnipotent God who does not even take care that his intentions shall be understood by his creatures,—could he be a God of goodness ? A God, who for thousands of years has permitted innumerable doubts and scruples to continue unchecked as if they were of no importance in the salvation of mankind, and who, nevertheless, announces the most dreadful consequences for anyone who mistakes his truth,— would he not be a cruel God if, being himself in possession of the truth, he could calmly contemplate mankind, in a state of miserable torment, worrying its mind as to what was truth ? "

" The Christian concept of God—God as the deity of the sick, God as spider, God as spirit—is one of the most corrupt concepts of God that has ever been attained on earth. Maybe it represents the low-water mark in the evolutionary ebb of the godlike type. God degenerated into the *contradiction of life*, instead of being its trans-figuration and eternal Yea ! "

Nietzsche's Verdict.—It is impossible within the limited space of this book to register all the criticisms Nietzsche levels at various other aspects of the phenomenon Christianity. Not that he overlooks the advantages of religion. According to him, in the hands of the strong, the masters, " religion is an additional means for overcoming resistance in the exercise of authority ; " in the mind of ordinary men, the majority of the people, who " exist for service and general utility, religion produces peace of heart and ennoblement of obedience, something of transfiguration and justifica-tion of all the commonplaceness, all the meanness, all the semi-animal poverty of their souls." But the Christian religion is to him, the apostle of the fuller life, *the* bugbear. He places it on the same level as Anarchism and Socialism, which, as he holds, are the fruits of the Christian doctrine of slaves. The New Testament he will not touch without gloves on his hands. His fury is lashed into frenzy when he studies the contemporary Christian. " The Christian *behaves* as all the world does, and *professes* a Christianity of ceremonies and states of soul. The man of to-day,—I am asphyxiated by his foul breath. Towards the past I exercise a sort of generous self-control, I take care not to hold mankind responsible for its mental dis-orders. But my feeling suddenly changes and vents itself the moment I enter the modern age, our age. It is indecent nowadays to be a Christian."

And with a volcanic eruption, he who called himself " the most essential opponent of Christianity " concludes and pronounces his judgment : " I *condemn* Christianity, and confront it with the most terrible accusation that an accuser has ever had in his mouth. To my mind it is the greatest of all conceivable corruptions. I call Christianity the one great curse, the one enormous and innermost perversion, the one great instinct of revenge, for which no means are too venomous, too underhand, too underground, and too *petty*— I call it the one immortal blemish of mankind ! "

CHAPTER IV

THE SUPERMAN

Principles.—The palæontologist Ludwig Rütimeyer, who, as a professor of zoology and comparative anatomy of the University of Bâle, was one of Nietzsche's colleagues, exercised considerable influence over him. With Rütimeyer he held that the present anthropoid monkeys and present man were two divergent branches from the same stem. Nietzsche even ventured to suggest that in order to prove the truth of this theory experiments ought to be arranged on a large scale and extending over millenniums.

With the exception of Rütimeyer, all the biologists whose works Nietzsche had read believed in the inheritability of newly-acquired characters. So it is no wonder that Nietzsche accepted this theory. Unfortunately, he often attributed to this heredity a scope and a speed which are not justified by facts.

Though he perceived, as we still do, that nobody as yet really knows what *is* that phenomenon called heredity, yet, in spite of one or two passages to the contrary, his writings amply prove his belief that conscious and artificial selection would be of great value to man, who has created, in civilisation as it is, a dangerous counter-agent and impediment to natural selection. " Man can henceforth make of himself what he desires ! "

With words like these he attempts to induce society to bring order into the almost hopeless chaos and absurd haphazard methods of our time.

Nietzsche's strongest point lies in his attitude towards Negative Eugenics. He advocates the elimination of the unfit and prohibition of offspring to certain people, *e.g.* syphilitics and criminals, two categories which in some American states have already been made harmless through legislation. Scientifically, little has been done or could be done by Nietzsche in Positive Eugenics. But some of his suggestions for improving the present marriage system are not without value.

The Superman, as an ideal standard to be attained by breeding, would come under the heading of Positive Eugenics. Since, however, no details referring to qualities are given by Nietzsche, the concept of the Superman is scientifically useless for the present, though it will undoubtedly exercise a great spiritual influence on man as a stimulus to action.

The word " Übermensch " (Over-man, Super-man) occurs as early as 1688, when it was used in a homily. Nietzsche probably picked up the word from Goethe. The famous philosopher, E. G. Dühring, in his work *The Value of Life*, 1865, points out that the evolution of man tends towards the transition into a finer and different species. It is more than probable that Nietzsche annexed this idea from Dühring.

Sometimes Nietzsche believed that the genius, the hero, is a sudden appearance, a lucky stroke, something like the mutations of De Vries, and this belief colours some of the statements about the Superman. On the whole, however, Nietzsche held that a slow and gradual transformation was the rule. Consequently, since a long time will necessarily elapse before the final appearance of the Superman, he thought out several intermediate stages. From the large basis of the present mankind will rise and *is* rising a variety : an aristocracy, strong in body and mind, which will rule the masses of Europe. From this new variety will spring a new race : the pure European race, Nietzsche's

" Higher Men." From these " Higher Men " will spring a new type, a new species : the Superman. " *Our Way,*" says Nietzsche, " *goes upwards from species to super-species !* "

The Exact Sciences and Man's Body.—" Too long the world has been a madhouse. Fortunately things are changing for the better. But modern man is still a short-sighted, stupid, selfish being. Having ceased to hold metaphysical views, he looks upon his short span of life too exclusively, and receives no strong incentives to build durable institutions intended to last for centuries—he himself wishes to pluck the fruit from the tree which he plants, and therefore he no longer plants those trees which require regular care for centuries, and which are destined to afford shade to a long series of generations. Modern man becomes smaller and ever smaller : the reason of it is the doctrine of happiness. Round, fair, and considerate are modern men to one another, as grains of sand are round, fair, and considerate to grains of sand. And so they muddle along without aim and without final purpose. But what we need are conquerors who do not believe in chance, but will bend it according to their will."

" The exact sciences triumph to-day—that is, those sciences that have accepted the evidence of our senses ; branches of knowledge such as metaphysics, theology, psychology, epistemology, or formal science, or a doctrine of symbols, like logic, and its applied form mathematics, are abortive and not yet science. In all these things reality does not come into consideration at all, even as a problem. But at any rate *there is hope in the exact sciences, and most of all in biology.* We know that even reason and logic are but higher spiritual shapes in the development of the physiological function of digestion, which compels an organism to make things ' like ' (to assimilate) before it can absorb them." How firmly Nietzsche believed in physiology we see in his words: " Much more than in the too palpably clumsy solution of things called God I am interested in another question—I refer to nutrition, a question

upon which the 'salvation of humanity' depends
to a far greater degree. Body am I entirely, and
nothing more ; and soul is only the name of something
in the body. Behind thy thoughts and feelings, my
brother, there is a mighty lord, an unknown sage—it
is called Self ; it dwelleth in thy body, it is thy body."
(This reminds one of Spencer's words, " To be a good
animal is the first requisite to success in life, and to be
a nation of good animals is the first condition of national
prosperity.") "That which is called 'flesh' and
'body' is of such incalculably greater importance that
the rest is nothing more than a small appurtenance.
To continue the chain of life so that it becomes even
more powerful—that is the task." And the stimulating ideal which Nietzsche created in this chain of life
is his ideal of the Superman.

The Gospel of the Superman.—" I teach you the
Superman. Man is something that is to be surpassed.
What have ye done to surpass man ? All beings
hitherto have created something beyond themselves,
and ye want to be the ebb of that great tide, and would
rather go back to the beast than surpass man ? What
is the ape to man ? A laughing-stock, a thing of shame.
And just the same shall man be to the Superman : a
laughing-stock, a thing of shame."

" The Superman is the meaning of the earth. Let
your will say : the Superman *shall be* the meaning of
the earth ! I conjure you, my brethren, *remain true
to the earth,* and believe not those who speak unto you
of super-earthly hopes ! Poisoners are they, whether
they know it or not."

" Man is a rope stretched between the animal and
the Superman—a rope over an abyss. A dangerous
crossing, a dangerous wayfaring, a dangerous looking-
back, a dangerous trembling and halting."

" I love him who liveth in order to know, and seeketh
to know in order that the Superman may hereafter
live. I love him who laboureth and investeth that he
may build the house for the Superman, and prepare
for him earth, animal, and plant. So I am a herald of

the lightning, and a heavy drop out of the cloud : the lightning, however, is the Superman."

What is Life ?—In order better to understand Nietzsche's dream-ideal, it is advisable to consider his views on What is Life ?   He gave several explanations. " It is a plurality of forces bound by a common nutritive process ;   a lasting form of force-establishing processes in which the various contending forces on their part grow unequally ;   it is *not* the continuous adjustment of internal relations to external relations, but will to power, which, proceeding from inside, subjugates and incorporates an ever-increasing quantity of external phenomena ;   it is *essentially* appropriation, injury, conquest of the strange and weak, suppression, severity, obtrusion of its own forms, incorporation, and at least, putting it mildest, exploitation ;   life is essentially amoral."   Of course these definitions are just as inadequate as any other definitions of life hitherto advanced.   Our imperfect knowledge as to the constitution and working of living matter has till now made it impossible to find an inclusive definition of life.   As usual, so Nietzsche's definitions, too, only shift the mystery.   But they are at least part of the truth.

Eternal Recurrence.—Another concept of Nietzsche which we must not disregard before approaching the details of his Superman concept and his Eugenics ideas is that of the Eternal Recurrence, which may be regarded as an antithesis to the Superman idea.   According to Nietzsche, " The universe is a monster of energy without beginning or end.   It is nothing vague, and does not stretch into infinity, but it is a definite quantum of energy located in limited space ;   the play of forces and force-waves, at the same time one and many, agglomerating here and diminishing there, a sea of forces storming and raging in itself, for ever hanging, for ever rolling back over incalculable ages to recurrence with an ebb and flow of its forms."   This concept of the universe, arising from the influence of Heraclitus on Nietzsche, led the latter to the concept of the Eternal Recurrence.

He thought he had discovered something brand new, and he became almost intoxicated with what he thought a unique discovery; this of course was foolish, for a similar idea can be encountered even amongst the old Babylonians and the Egyptians. Nietzsche conceived the universe as " a definite quantity of energy, as a definite number of centres of energy—and every other concept remains indefinite and therefore useless; it follows therefrom that the universe must go through a calculable number of combinations in the great game of chance which constitutes its existence. In infinity, at some moment or other, every possible combination must once have been realised; not only this, but it must have been realised an infinite number of times. And inasmuch as between every one of these combinations and its next recurrence every other possible combination would necessarily have been undergone, and since every one of these combinations would determine the whole series in the same order, a circular movement of absolutely identical series is thus demonstrated : the universe is thus shown to be a circular movement which has already repeated itself an infinite number of times, and which plays its game for all eternity. This conception is *not simply materialistic*, for if it were it would not involve an infinite recurrence of identical cases but a finite state. That a state of equilibrium has never been reached proves that it is impossible. If the universe had a goal, that goal would have been reached by now. If any sort of unforeseen final state existed, that state also would have been reached. Owing to the fact that the universe has not reached this final state, materialism shows itself to be but an imperfect and provisional hypothesis."

Thus Nietzsche's concept was not apparently a mere mechanical idea, but participated somewhat of a transcendental character. At any rate his sister scorns the idea that her brother's concept of the Eternal Recurrence was similar to that of the Pythagoreans. But it remains a cloudy vision, a last yearning to retain the beautiful dream of immortality, a stumbling-block to the realisation of the Superman concept. If we assume time to be infinite and an infinite number of centres of energy to exist, Eternal Recurrence is impossible. If, with Nietzsche, we assume time to be infinite and a finite number of such centres, Eternal Recurrence, as every mathematician can calculate, is highly improbable. On the other hand, it is worth mentioning that Frederick Soddy, in his book *The Interpretation of Radium* (1909), says: " *The idea that evolution is proceeding in continuous cycles*, without beginning and without end, in which the waste energy of one part of the cycle is transformed in another part of the cycle into available forms, is at least as *possible and conceivable* in the present state of knowledge as the older idea, which was based on a too wide application of those laws of the availability of energy we have found to hold within our own experience."

Why did Nietzsche cling to this peculiar idea ? He preached the " Amor Fati," that is, how to love and say Yea to fate. To him it was a justification of life even where it is most terrible. He thought the Eternal Recurrence to be of a disciplinary, chastening influence ; a test for the character and courage of his " Higher Men," who were not only " not to shun life like pessimists, but who, just as revellers at a banquet desire their cups refilled, will say to life : Once again ! "

Nietzsche would have had great difficulty to prove that the centres of energy in space are limited. His definition of life is a stimulating thought for those who dream of the future greatness of man, of the Eugenists' Utopia, of the Superman ; if it is appropriation, conquest of the strange and weak, suppression, man will appropriate the rule of the mechanical universe, conquer that ancient and obstinate libertine Nature, and suppress all that is hostile to life. But Nietzsche's Eternal Recurrence is an oppressive, a paralysing thought to those hopeful dreamers ; if there is no goal at all, what is the good of anything, of the Superman, of a freer morality ?—Nietzsche's æsthetic-phenomenon-theory of the world, which has already been mentioned, would of course refute the necessity of a goal. But man gets tired of everlasting lovely sunsets and clever games of chess if no promise, no hope, no end is imaginable.

If some writers on Nietzsche consider the Eternal Recurrence, as he himself sometimes does, to be the essential item, the fundamental idea in his doctrines, they are mistaken. What will live of Nietzsche long after his Eternal Recurrence has been forgotten is his beautiful idea of the Superman. This idea, by the way, as far as Nietzsche goes, is older; it can be traced in some form or other even in his very first books, whereas the Eternal Recurrence did not occur to him till 1881. And it is worth recording that Nietzsche once remarked himself, " Eternal Recurrence is the worst form of Nihilism."

Need of a Goal.—" We live in the Atomic Age, or rather in the Atomic Chaos. The opposing forces were practically held together in mediæval times by the Church, and in some measure assimilated by the strong pressure which she exerted. When the common tie broke and the pressure relaxed, these forces rose once more against each other." Now we have Evolution instead of the Church. " Evolution does not make happiness its goal; it aims merely at evolution and nothing else. *It is only if humanity had a universally recognised goal that we could propose to do this or that ; for the time being there is no such goal.* If mankind in general agreed to adopt such a goal, it could then impose a moral law upon itself, a law which would, at all events, be imposed by its own free will." That self-set goal is the Superman ; that self-imposed morality is that mode of conduct which will evolve from Eugenics considerations. Of course Nietzsche never used the word Eugenics. The scientific crystallisation of Nietzsche's dream we find in Sir Francis Galton's work.

Changes in the Superman-Idea.—The concept of the Superman underwent many changes in Nietzsche's mind. At first he was sure it was to be one great *individual*. Perhaps no name recurs more frequently in Nietzsche's writings than that of Napoleon. Nietzsche's need of hero-worship can be traced throughout his life. Now it is Schopenhauer, who appeared to him to be " the great synthetic power " in our " atomic age," a " simplifier of the universe " ; now it is Wagner, who is to be the " educator of mankind."

As early as 1874 Nietzsche asked, " Who will set up again the *Image of Man*, when men in their selfishness and terror see nothing but the trail of the serpent or the cur in them, and have fallen from their high estate to that of the brute or the automaton ? There are three images of man fashioned by our modern time, which for a long while yet will urge mortal men to transfigure their own lives ; they are the men of Rousseau, Goethe, and Schopenhauer. The first has the greatest fire, and is most calculated to impress the people; the second is only for the few, for those contemplative natures " in the grand style " who are misunderstood by the crowd. The third demands the highest activity in those who will follow it : only active men will look on that image without harm, for it breaks the spirit of the merely contemplative man and the rabble shudder at it." As can be seen from the last words quoted, amongst these three early prototypes of the Superman, the third, the Schopenhauer-man, is the one most favoured by Nietzsche. And many traits in the character of his poetical figure Zarathustra show resemblance to his Schopenhauer-man, who " voluntarily takes upon himself the pain of telling the truth."

It is really love's labour lost to attempt finding an exact statement in Nietzsche's books as to what he really meant by the Superman. Just as little as a Socialist can give an account of the real details and facts of his ideal, just as little could the anti-socialist, the aristocratic Nietzsche, give of his. He says, " Not mankind but *Superman* is the goal ! " He fights that " idealism " which will make everything uniform, he hates " that stationary level of mankind where economical consumption of men and mankind, an ever more closely involved ' machinery ' of interests and services, result in stultification, higher Chinese culture, modesty in

the instincts " ; he believes that with such a levelling
process is inevitably associated a counter movement
which he calls the " separation of the *luxurious surplus
of mankind.*" " By means of it a stronger kind, a
higher type, must come to light, which has other conditions for its origin and for its maintenance than the
average man. *My concept, my metaphor for this type, is
the word Superman. Upwards goes our way from species
to super-species.*" So, whereas at first we found in
Nietzsche's mind a Superman concept which resembled
Carlyle's and Emerson's ideal figures, our Eugenic poet-
philosopher now speaks of a higher *type,* a higher species.
The idealism and verbalism of the classical scholar and
philologist created in the seventies the Individual-Super-
man ; the realism of the disillusioned man, who found
in biology a friendly cheering goddess, created in the
eighties the Higher Type Superman. Instead of a Superman like Napoleon, a superior type of men is posited.

The strong belief that the Superman—this Antichrist
and Antinihilist, this conqueror of God and of Nothing-
ness—*must* one day come, did not always prevail in
Nietzsche's mind. There came doubts. He remembers
the foolish belief of man as to his self-importance, when,
" as astronomers tell us, life on earth has no significance
for the whole, that life probably everywhere is but a
flicker, an instant, with long, long intervals afterwards,
that the earth, like every star, is but a hiatus between
two nonentities." He denies that he has any intention
of improving mankind ; he does not want to set up any
new idols, and declares that the overthrowing of idols—
i.e. all ideals—is much more his business.

Religious Aspect of the Superman-Idea.—In details
Nietzsche's Superman affords very little help ; but the
general idea of it, embodying as it does the metaphysical
hopes of all the best religions and ethical systems,
strikes a note which cannot fail to assist mankind, just
coming of age, in realising the great possibilities of the
future. It is a life-furthering idea. Nietzsche, through
this concept of the Superman, wants people to hate
everything that makes for weakness and exhaustion,

and to favour every action that will increase man's strength and power. The Will to Power is the driving force of the Superman ; he does not want contentment but more power, he prefers war to a dishonourable peace.

Though this Superman of Nietzsche's is but a cloudy vision and an uncertain ideal, it is decidedly a noble and stimulating one. If our contemporaries, the Pragmatists, hold that life and action are the greatest things, if the Activism of Eucken asks us to set our aims towards " the highest " in order to share the Universal Spiritual Life, where can we find a better life than that which the Superman demands, when we are asked by Nietzsche to sacrifice ourselves to prepare the way for creatures which stand sublimely above the whole species of man ? Where a purer mode of action than the fidelity and unselfishness needed to make future generations happier and better than we are ? The ideal of the Superman establishes for the present generation an active and, moreover, an anti-egoistic, an altruistic morality, inasmuch as individuals have to devote themselves entirely to the furtherance of an aim which they in their own personality will never attain.—That he permits to the greater number of present mankind a too limited egoism, and demands from them—the " slaves "—*nothing but altruism*, nothing but self-sacrifice for the sake of the Superman, in this lies a dangerous error of Nietzsche's.

He desired to promote the victory of a pure and carefully executed system of Darwinian ethics over that of the " culture-Philistines " and of Christianity. But he added to the evolutionist's egoism an ideal altruism adopted from Christianity. He did so because the religious element formed a powerful component in his doctrine of the Superman.

Sir Francis Galton says : " Eugenics must be introduced into the national conscience like a new religion. It has, indeed, strong claims to become an orthodox religious tenet of the future. I see no impossibility in Eugenics becoming a religious dogma among mankind." And Zarathustra, who was thirty years old when he left his home and went into the mountains to enjoy his spirit, and his solitude, and for ten years did not weary of it, Zarathustra said of the priests, " My blood is related to theirs ; and I want, withal, my blood honoured in theirs ! "—" By still greater ones than any of the Saviours must ye be saved, my brethren, if ye would find the way to freedom ! Never yet hath there been a Superman." On another occasion we find Zarathustra exclaiming, " What must one day come and may not pass by ? Our great Hazar, that is to say, our great, remote human-kingdom, the Zarathustra-kingdom of a thousand years."

Nietzsche, the contemporary of Sir Francis Galton, Nietzsche, a pioneer of Eugenics, he too had perceived that the prophet and the poet, the enthusiast and the seer are far more faithfully and loyally followed than the thinker and the scholar ; so it was likewise clear to him that an approximation of his ideals to those of religion made them so much the more alluring and attractive. Nietzsche was the son of a parson.

The absolute obligation, the categorical imperative, the inspiring ardour which are inseparable from the highest religious aims, all these Nietzsche desired for his ideal. Just as the religious man is ready to sacrifice all for his God, and fixes his gaze solely upon Him, so also should present humanity be disposed to devote all to the Superman, and spread out the wings of desire towards him alone.

And *Nietzsche believed in law and order*, in evolution through law and order. H. G. Wells has written a novel, *The New Machiavelli*, one of the finest novels ever written. There we have a hero who wants to make future generations happier, and is full of " fine thinking " about Eugenics measures and social reform. But he fails because he lacks the necessary self-discipline and respect of the law. And here may be stated one of the most fundamental aspects of Nietzsche's teaching, one of the most fruitful rules of conduct to be derived from his writings : To the reformer, the pioneer, in order to fight his way out of the chaos, a certain *disciplinary constraint* is necessary. A man has to choose between either going to the dogs or prevailing. He must be capable of the greatest hardness towards himself ; he must possess the most enduring will power. —"*He who cannot command himself shall obey !* "

Eugenics.—Nietzsche did not know the word Eugenics, but the founder of the science of Eugenics, Sir Francis Galton, was not an unknown name to him. Nietzsche read *Inquiries into Human Faculty and its Development* in 1884, and the idea of the slaves and the herds, later on so predominant in Nietzsche's writings, may have been helped on not a little by this passage in Galton's book :
" . . . *slavish* aptitudes from which the leaders of men are exempt, but which are characteristic elements in the disposition of ordinary persons. The vast majority of persons of our race have a natural tendency to shrink from the responsibility of standing and acting alone ; they exalt the *vox populi*, even when they know it to be the utterance of a *mob* of nobodies, into the *vox dei*, and they are willing slaves to tradition, authority, and custom. . . . This hereditary taint, due to the primæval barbarism of our race, and maintained by later influences, will have to be bred out of it before our descendants can rise to the position of free members of an intelligent society. . . ."

There is a wealth of Eugenics material scattered throughout Nietzsche's writings. Only a few most salient points can be collected here. The future is ours, not the past. " To redeem what is past and to transform every ' It was ' into ' Thus would I have it ! ' that only do I call redemption." He wants men " to choose that path which man hath followed blindly, and to approve of it—and no longer to slink aside from it like the sick and perishing ! " Then we shall be able to fight the giants Chance and Nonsense, both of which have ruled mankind till now.

" Tell me, my brother, what do we think bad, and worst of all ? Is it not degeneration ? Upwards goes our way from species to super-species. But a horror to us is the degenerating sense, which saith :

All for myself." To fight such degeneration Nietzsche insists that the legislator ought to consider the welfare of the race above that of the individual, the interests of the coming centuries more than the petty sufferings of his contemporaries. The administrator ought to husband his strength for great monumental tasks, and not to fritter it away with innumerable paltry deeds of pity. "Thus demandeth my great love to the remotest ones : *be not considerate of thy neighbour !* Man is something that must be surpassed."

"Suffering is the source of greatness !" Again and again in Nietzsche's writings recurs the idea that the production of genius is very often conditioned by an unfavourable environment. Such unfavourable conditions make the type a strong and stable type. Venice became strong through the constant struggle with her neighbours. And so Nietzsche preaches : "Become hard !"

Nietzsche was, on the whole, inclined towards the school of Lamarck. He believed in the possible inheritance of acquired qualities. This accounts for a passage in which he almost contradicts what he said about the beneficent influence of unfavourable environment. "Wealth necessarily creates an aristocracy of race, for it permits the choice of the most beautiful women and the engagement of the best teachers ; it allows a man cleanliness, time for physical exercise, and, above all, immunity from dulling physical labour. So far it provides all the conditions for making man, after a few generations, move and even act nobly and handsomely." From the point of view of the present state of knowledge these assumptions of Nietzsche are very doubtful indeed !

At other times, however, he stressed the innate hereditary factor and approaches Mendelism. "*Everything good is an inheritance ; that which is not inherited is imperfect : it is simply a beginning.*" The beauty, charm, and perfection of a race or of a family is attained with pains : like genius, it is the final result of the accumulated work of generations. Good things are exceedingly costly : and in all cases the law obtains that he who possesses them is a different person from him who is *acquiring* them. " A man may be justly proud of an unbroken line of *good* ancestors down to his father. Descent from good ancestors constitutes the real nobility of birth ; a single break in the chain, one bad ancestor, therefore, destroys the nobility of birth." In spite of various attacks on Darwin, Nietzsche agrees with him on " the greater importance of the nature of the organism over the nature of the conditions." Quite Mendelian is Nietzsche's argument which goes for some modern educational theories trying to get grapes from a bush of thorns, a silk purse from a sow's ear. " With the help of the best education and culture. one will only succeed in *deceiving* with regard to such heredity ! It is quite impossible for a man *not* to have the qualities and predilections of his parents and ancestors in his constitution, whatever appearances may suggest to the contrary. This is the problem of the race."

For Darwin's struggle for existence Nietzsche substitutes a struggle for power. The struggle for existence, according to him, is an exception, the general condition of life is not one of want or famine, but rather of riches, of lavish luxuriance, and even of absurd prodigality.

Very interesting as an illustration of Nietzsche's shrewdness is a passage complaining that heredity and environment, after all, are merely words, and do not explain anything that really matters. They are only designations for the identification of a problem. " *How* a given organ gets to be used for any particular purpose is not explained. There is just as little explained in regard to these things by the assumption of *causæ finales* as by the assumption of *causæ efficientes*." Amongst the most valuable of Nietzsche's contributions to Eugenics are his opinions on marriage.

Marriage.—Nietzsche is often referred to as an enemy of women. In his *Zarathustra* is a line which is often quoted : " Thou goest to women ? Do not forget thy whip ! " But the same man also wrote, " One cannot be gentle enough towards women ! " and " *The perfect* *woman is a higher type of humanity than the perfect man, and also something much rarer."*

There is too much left to chance and hazard in modern marriages. " All rationality of a great advance on humanity is rendered impossible by the hazard of marriages." Love is almost absent in the bourgeois marriages. " The whole matter consists in society giving leave to two persons to satisfy their sexual desires under conditions obviously designed to safeguard social order. The old nobility understood by marriage the breeding and maintenance of a fixed definite type of ruler. What people, however, call ' love matches ' nowadays have error for their father and need for their mother."

A man should not marry unless he knows he is sound, of good ancestry, and entitled to desire a child. " Beyond thyself shalt thou build. But first of all must thou be built thyself, rectangular in body and soul. Not only onward shalt thou propagate thyself but *upward !* For that purpose may the garden of marriage help thee ! *Marriage ;* so call I the will of the twain to create the one that is more than those who created it. The reverence for one another, as those exercising such a will, call I marriage."

Besides such a self-examination the prospective candidate for marriage ought to ask himself whether he has a talent for friendship, because a good marriage is based on that talent ; he ought to ask himself the question : " Do you think you will pass your time well with this woman till your old age ? " All else in marriage is transitory ; talk, however, occupies most of the time of association.

Like Meredith who, by the way, was an ardent Eugenist, conscious of man's obligations to the future, and who sang :—

> " Life begets with fair increase
> *Beyond the flesh*, if life be true ! "

like him, and like some American legislators, Nietzsche favours a trial-marriage. People who are badly paired become revengeful and spiteful if the tie cannot be loosened. " Marriage-breaking is better than marriage-bending, marriage-lying."—" A set term and ' small marriage ' will enable people to see whether their love will last, and whether they are fit for the great marriage."

Our passions must be our servants. Voluptuousness is to free hearts " a thing innocent and free, the garden-happiness of the earth, all the future's thanks-overflow to the present," but to the rabble it is " the slow fire at which it is burnt."

The future marriage ought to be a spiritual friendship ; " contracted for the purpose of producing and educating a new generation—such marriage which only makes use of the sensual, so to speak, as a rare and occasional means to a higher purpose will, it is to be feared, probably need a natural auxiliary, namely, *concubinage*. For if, on the grounds of his health, the wife is also to serve for the sole satisfaction of the man's sexual needs, a wrong perspective, opposed to the aims indicated, will have most influence in the choice of a wife. The aim referred to—the production of descendants—will be accidental, and the successful education of these descendants highly improbable."

Curious and decidedly sound are some detailed suggestions of Nietzsche's concerning the future of marriage. He demands (1) a *supertax* on inherited property and a longer term of military service for bachelors ; (2) a *medical certificate* as a condition of any marriage, endorsed by the parish authorities, in which a series of questions addressed to the parties and the medical officers must be answered (family histories) ; (3) *privileges* of all sorts for fathers who contribute a numerous male offspring to the community ; and perhaps plural votes as well ; (4) *leasehold marriages* for a term of years or months (with adequate provision for the children) as a counter-agent to prostitution, or as its ennoblement ; (5) every marriage to be warranted and sanctioned by a certain number of good men and true of the parish, as an affair which concerns the parish ; (6) *prohibition of offspring to the unfit.*

The last point, which claims so much attention nowadays, and has led in California, Connecticut, Indiana, Iowa, Nevada, New Jersey, and New York already to legislation, may be further elucidated by these words of Nietzsche : " There are cases where to have a child would be a crime—for example, for chronic invalids and extreme neurasthenics. One of the regular symptoms of exhausted stock is the inability to exercise any self-restraint in the presence of stimuli, and the tendency to respond to the smallest sexual attraction. In such cases the priest and moralist play a hopeless game. It is a question for the doctor. *Society has here a positive duty to fulfil, and of all the demands that are made on it there are few more urgent and necessary than this one.* Society, as the trustee of life, is responsible for every botched life *before* it comes into existence, and as society has to suffer for such lives it *ought*, consequently, to be made impossible for them ever to see the light of day. Society *should* in many cases actually prevent the act of procreation, and may, without any regard for rank, descent, or intellect, hold in readiness the most rigorous forms of compulsion and restriction, and, under certain circumstances, have recourse to sterilisation."

" The Mosaic law, ' Thou shalt do no murder,' is a piece of childish *naïveté* compared with the seriousness of telling decadents, ' Thou shalt not beget ' ! ! ! . . . . For Life itself recognises no solidarity or equality of rights between the healthy and unhealthy parts of an organism. The latter must, at all costs, be *eliminated* lest the whole should perish. Compassion for decadents, equal rights for the physiologically botched —this would be the very pinnacle of immorality, it would be setting up Nature's most formidable opponent as morality itself ! "

The United States of Europe.—Some of these views concerning future marriages propounded by Nietzsche will seem rather advanced or Utopian to the reader ;

with others he will be already conversant. But we must realise that the above passages were written almost thirty years ago, long before Eugenics came to the fore. Naturally, Nietzsche guessed that it would take a long time before any such reforms might be tackled. And so he set to work to attack many things which he considered stumbling-blocks in the way of progress.

It is certain that all thorough-going Eugenics reforms can be established only when we know more than we do now about that mysterious phenomenon called " heredity " ; it is more than probable that they will have to wait till what Nietzsche called the conversion of " a moral mankind into a wise mankind " has taken place, till women as well as men are economically independent, till, above all, the foolish and futile aspirations of national narrow-mindedness with its parish-pump jingoism, with its ridiculous and antediluvian war-mania has been thrown on the rubbish-heap and all the freed expenditure for armaments will be spent on education—Eugenics education above all—and social amelioration. Nietzsche inveighed against the last-mentioned stumbling-block—nationalism. Once or twice he referred indirectly to a future earth-state in which the whole planet will be ruled by a wise mankind. But as that lies rather in a dim future, he threw himself whole-heartedly into a campaign to advocate " A United Europe."

" A little more fresh air, for Heaven's sake ! This ridiculous condition of Europe *must* not last any longer. *Is there a single idea behind this bovine nationalism ?* What positive value can there be in encouraging this arrogant self-conceit when everything to-day points to greater and more common interests ?—at a moment when the spiritual dependence and denationalisation, which are obvious to all, are paving the way for the reciprocal *rapprochements* and fertilisations which make up the real value and sense of present-day culture ? The economic unity of Europe must come."

" Owing to the morbid estrangement which the nationality-craze has induced and still induces among the nations of Europe, owing also to the short-sighted and hasty-handed politicians who, with the help of this craze, are at present in power, and do not suspect to what extent the disintegrating policy they pursue must necessarily be only an interlude policy,—owing to all this, and much else that is altogether unmention-able at present, the most unmistakable signs that *Europe wishes to be one,* are now overlooked or arbi-trarily and falsely misinterpreted. With all the more profound and large-minded men of this century, the real general tendency of the mysterious labour of their souls was to prepare the way for that new synthesis and tentatively to anticipate the European of the future; only in their simulations or in their weaker moments, in old age perhaps, did they belong to the ' fatherlands '—they only rested from themselves when they became ' patriots.' I think of such men as Napoleon, Goethe, Beethoven, Stendhal, Heinrich Heine, Schopenhauer."

Nietzsche does not give any satisfactory indications as to how the United States of Europe might be brought about. In one place he says that the overwhelming power and threatening attitude of Russia might perhaps compel Europe to abandon the comedy of petty politics and unite against that semi-barbarous country. Our philosopher revels in calling himself and those of a similar bent of mind " European." " We are not nearly ' German ' enough to advocate nationalism and race hatred, or take delight in the national heart-itch and blood-poisoning, on account of which the nations of Europe are at present bounded off and secluded from one another as if by quarantines. We are too unpre-judiced for that, too perverse, too fastidious; also too well-informed and too much ' travelled.' We are, in a word—and it shall be our word of honour!—*good Europeans,* the heirs of Europe, the rich, over-wealthy heirs, also the too deeply-pledged heirs of millenniums of European thought."

Education.—The " United Europe " was, in the soul of our poet-philosopher, one of the dimly perceived pathways which might lead to his Eugenics kingdom, where the policy of an ascending life sways the whole realm of human thought and action, where the Superman might become an idea within the radius of faith. Another pathway to his kingdom Nietzsche perceived in education—perhaps, in the long run, the safest and surest way for all reformers ! Educate the young and educate public opinion !

This great interest in education is quite natural in Nietzsche, who was a professor and a teacher—who already, as a young man of twenty-eight, tried in his five lectures on *The Future of our Educational Institutions* to outline a new and better system of education. Quite in accordance with his later-developed aristocratic views on masters and slaves, he says somewhere in these lectures : " The education of the masses cannot, therefore, be our aim ; but rather the education of a few picked men for great and lasting work." Nietzsche objects to the prevalence of verbalism in schools, to the preponderance of philologists in our schools. Philologists, in his opinion, stand in the same relation to true educators as the medicine-men of the wild Indian to true physicians. He says that purely philological (linguistic) studies result in arrogant expectation, culture-Philistinism, superficiality, and too high esteem for reading and writing. " The young *students should be brought into contact with exact sciences and with real art !* "

Higher Men.—The United States of Europe, a superior education, are good and valuable means to attain the goal, but, after all, they are only like the shell and like the sustenance ; what is needed is the substance, **Men.** Nietzsche felt that the Superman was an ill-defined though beautiful, a transcendental though fascinating, *ideal.* And for once Nietzsche became practical, and outlined a policy to create a race of men superior to the majority of present mankind, his Higher Men. And here, where he deals with a practicable policy, can be found many a valuable hint, many a stimulating thought, many a great guiding maxim.

Of course his policy is that of the aristocrat, for the

few. " On great leaders, great individuals, mankind
will always have to depend for its ideal, although con-
tinually trying to dispense with great individuals by
means of corporations, &c." These great individuals,
these higher men, will in the future *change mankind from
a moral into a wise mankind.* When they have done
that, the life-purpose of the higher men is fulfilled ;
they are only bridges to the Superman, they are only
transitions.

But brave pioneers they needs must be, these higher
men ; men, " silent, solitary, and resolute, who know
how to be content and persistent in invisible activity ;
men who, with innate disposition, seek in all things
that which is to be overcome in them ; men to whom
cheerfulness, patience, simplicity, and contempt of the
great vanities belong, just as much as do magnanimity
in victory and indulgence, to the trivial vanities of all
the vanquished ; men accustomed to command with
perfect assurance, and equally ready, if need be, to
obey—proud in the one case as in the other, equally
serving their own interests ; men more imperilled,
more productive, more happy ! "

The " aristocracy of good Europeans " will be less
ashamed of their instincts. They will be atheists and
immoralists, but take care to support the religions and
the morality of the masses. " Beyond Good and Evil—
certainly ; but we Good Europeans insist upon the unconditional and strict preservation of herd-morality.
Detached, well-to-do, strong : irony concerning the
' press ' and its culture. We mistrust any form of
culture that tolerates newspaper reading or writing."

The " higher men " will be noble, *i.e.* they will be
fond of " external punctiliousness, of a slow step, a slow
glance, able to keep silence ; they will know how to
bear poverty, want, and even illness " ; they will be
capable " of leisure, of unconditional conviction that,
although a handicraft does not shame one in any sense,
it certainly reduces one's rank."—" Courtesy is one of
their greatest virtues." All these things, however, are
mere trifles compared with the next.

Self-discipline is the thing on which Nietzsche insists most, and next to self-discipline he puts before the higher men *obedience* and *fidelity!* "The only thing which to-day proves whether a man has any value or not is the capacity of sticking to his guns!"

And he will need these virtues, the higher man! The Philistines will oppose him, they who are the "barrier in the way of all powerful men and creators, the fetters of those who would run towards lofty goals, the poisonous mist that chokes all germinating hopes. The Philistines hate the dominating genius. They are a rabble in the market-place, and do not believe in higher men, but say: "We are all equal!" The higher men must surpass the Philistines' "petty virtues, the petty policy, the sand-grain considerateness, the ant-hill trumpery, the pitiable comfortableness, the happiness of the greatest number."

To do so the higher men need *hope, courage—illusions.* "Hedge yourselves with a great all-embracing hope, and strive on!" The higher men must be courageous and "fighters against their time." "In the present state of knowledge, illusions, logical fictions, false opinions (to which the synthetic judgments *a priori* belong) are the most indispensable to us; often more than truth they are life-furthering, life-preserving, species-preserving, perhaps species-rearing." But courage and hope rank first amongst the three. "By my love and hope I conjure thee: cast not away the hero in thy soul! Maintain holy thy highest hope!"

With all the fervour of the visionary, Nietzsche, the poet-philosopher, believes in the coming of the "higher men." "I greet all the signs indicating that a more manly and warlike age is commencing, which will, above all, bring heroism again into honour. For it has to prepare the way for a yet higher age, and gather the force which the latter will one day require—the age which will carry heroism into knowledge and *wage war* for the sake of ideas and their consequences."

With all the solemnity of an explorer annexing a newly-discovered isle and planting on it the flag of his king, Nietzsche, the finest pioneer Eugenics ever had, consecrates his new nobility of higher men :

" O, my brethren, I consecrate you and point you to a new nobility : ye shall become procreators and culti-vators and sowers of the future."

" Verily, not to a nobility which ye could purchase like traders with traders' gold ; for little worth is all that hath its price."

" *Let it not be your honour henceforth whence ye come, but whither ye go.*"

" O my brethren, not backward shall your nobility gaze, but *outward !* Exiles shall ye be from all father-lands and forefather lands ! "

" Your *children's land* shall ye love, let this love be your new nobility—the undiscovered in the remotest seas ! For it do I bid your sails search and search ! "

BIBLIOGRAPHY

A. ENGLISH

The Works of Friedrich Nietzsche—First complete English translation, in eighteen volumes. Edited by Dr. Oscar Levy. 1909–1913. Edinburgh and London, Foulis.

Chatterton-Hill, G., *The Philosophy of Nietzsche.* 1912. London, Ouseley ; pp. 292.

Common, Th., *Nietzsche as Critic, Philosopher, Poet, and Prophet.* 1901. London, Grant Richards ; pp. lxv +261.

Dolson, G. N., *The Philosophy of Friedrich Nietzsche.* 1901. New York, The Macmillan Company ; pp. v +110.

Foerster-Nietzsche, E., *The Young Nietzsche.* 1912. London, Heinemann ; pp. viii +399.

Gould, G. M., *Biographic Clinics.* 1904. London, Rehman ; vol. ii., pp. 283–322.

Halévy, D., *The Life of Friedrich Nietzsche.* 1911. London, Fisher Unwin ; pp. 368.

Havelock-Ellis, Mrs., *Three Modern Seers.* 1910. London, Stanley Paul & Co. ; pp. 155–89.

Kennedy, J. M., *The Quintessence of Nietzsche.* 1909. London, Werner Laurie ; pp. xiv +364.

Knapp, A. W., *Friedrich Nietzsche, a Plain Account of the Fiery Philosopher.* 1910. London, Watts and Co. ; pp. 20.

Levy, O., *The Revival of Aristocracy.* 1906. London, Probsthain ; pp. xiv +119.

Lichtenberger, H., *The Gospel of Superman.* 1910. London, Foulis ; pp. ix +222.

Ludovici, A. M., *Who is to be the Master of the World ?*
1909. London, Foulis ; pp. xii +199.
Ludovici, A. M., *Nietzsche, His Life and Works.* 1910.
London, Constable ; pp. xiii +102.
Ludovici, A. M., *Nietzsche and Art.* 1911. London,
Constable ; pp. xvi +236.
Mencken, H. L., *The Philosophy of Friedrich Nietzsche.*
1908. London, Fisher Unwin ; pp. xiv +321.
Mügge, M. A., *Friedrich Nietzsche, His Life and Work.*
1911. London, Fisher Unwin ; 3rd edition, pp.
xii +458.
Orage, A. R., *Friedrich Nietzsche : The Dionysian Spirit
of the Age.* 1906. London, Foulis ; pp. 83.
Orage, A. R., *Nietzsche in Outline and Aphorism.* 1907.
London, Foulis ; pp. 188.

B. Foreign

Meyer, R. M., *Nietzsche, Sein Leben und seine Werke.*
1913. München, Beck ; pp. x +702.
Richter, R., *Friedrich Nietzsche, Sein Leben und sein
Werk.* 1903. Leipsic, Dürr ; pp. vii +288.
Foerster, E. (Foerster-Nietzsche), *Das Leben Friedrich
Nietzsche's.* 1895–1904. Leipsic, Naumann ; 3 vols.,
pp. xxiii +1313.
Seillière, E., *Apollôn ou Dionysos.* 1905. Paris, Plon ;
pp. xxviii +364.
Faguet, E., *En lisant Nietzsche.* 1904. Paris, Société
française d'imprimerie ; pp. 362.
Zoccoli, E. G., *Friedrich Nietzsche.* 1901. Torino,
Fratelli Bocca ; pp. xvi +331.
Sanz y Escartin, Ed., *Friedrich Nietzsche y el anarquismo
intelectual.* 1898. Madrid, A. Garcia ; pp. 53

INDEX